Vocabulary
Power Plus
for the
ACT

Vocabulary,
Reading, and Writing
Exercises for High Scores

Book Two

By Daniel A. Reed

Edited by Paul Moliken

Prestwick House

P.O. Box 658 • Clayton, DE 19938
(800) 932-4593 • www.prestwickhouse.com

ISBN   978-1-935467-06-9

Vocabulary Power Plus for the ACT

Book Two

Vocabulary, Reading, and Writing Exercises for High Scores

Table of Contents

Vocabulary
Power Plus
for the ACT
Vocabulary,
Reading, and Writing
Exercises for High Scores

·Introduction·

Vocabulary Power Plus for the ACT combines classroom tested vocabulary drills with reading and writing exercises designed to prepare students for the American College Testing assessment; however, *Vocabulary Power Plus for the ACT* is a resource for all students—not just those who are college bound or preparing for the ACT. This series is intended to increase vocabulary, improve grammar, enhance writing, and boost critical–reading skills for students at all levels of learning.

Vocabulary lessons combine words-in-context exercises with inferences to ensure that definitions are understood, instead of merely memorized.

Lengthy critical reading exercises and detailed questions emulate the reading passages of the ACT Reading test. Each passage involves a topic in social studies, natural science, prose fiction, or humanities, and is accompanied by multiple levels of questions.

ACT-style grammar passages and questions provide practice in punctuation, usage, structure, and word choice.

The process-oriented writing exercises in *Vocabulary Power Plus for the ACT* develop speed and thrift in essay writing, qualifiable with the objective writing fundamentals in the simulated ACT essay scoring guide.

We hope that you find the *Vocabulary Power Plus for the ACT* series to be an effective tool for teaching new words and an exceptional tool for preparing for the ACT.

Strategies for Completing Activities

Roots, Prefixes, and Suffixes

A knowledge of roots, prefixes, and suffixes can give readers the ability to view unfamiliar words as puzzles that require only a few simple steps to solve. For the person interested in the history of words, this knowledge provides the ability to track word origin and evolution. For those who seek to improve vocabulary, this knowledge creates a sure and lifelong method; however, there are two points to remember:

1. Some words have evolved through usage, so present definitions might differ from what you infer through an examination of the roots and prefixes. The word *abstruse*, for example, contains the prefix *ab* (away) and the root *trudere* (to thrust), and literally means *to thrust away*. Today, *abstruse* is used to describe something that is hard to understand.

2. Certain roots do not apply to all words that use the same form. If you know that the root *vin* means "to conquer," then you would be correct in concluding that the word *invincible* means "incapable of being conquered"; however, if you tried to apply the same root meaning to *vindicate* or *vindictive*, you would be incorrect. When analyzing unfamiliar words, check for other possible roots if your inferred meaning does not fit the context.

Despite these considerations, a knowledge of roots and prefixes is one of the best ways to build a powerful vocabulary.

Critical Reading

Reading questions generally fall into several categories.

1. *Identifying the main idea or the author's purpose.* Generally, the question will ask, "What is this selection about?"

In some passages, the author's purpose will be easy to identify because one or two ideas leap from the text; however, other passages might not be so easily analyzed, especially if they include convoluted sentences. Inverted sentences (subject at the end of the sentence) and elliptical sentences (words missing) will also increase the difficulty of the passages, but all of these obstacles can be overcome if readers take one sentence at a time and recast it in their own words. Consider the following sentence:

> These writers either jot down their thoughts bit by bit, in short, ambiguous, and paradoxical sentences, which apparently mean much more than they say—of this kind of writing Schelling's treatises on natural philosophy are a splendid instance; or else they hold forth with a deluge of words and the most intolerable diffusiveness, as though no end of fuss were necessary to make the reader understand the deep meaning of their sentences, whereas it is some quite simple if not actually trivial idea, examples of which may be found in plenty in the popular works of Fichte, and the philosophical manuals of a hundred other miserable dunces.

If we edit out some of the words, the main point of this sentence is obvious.

> These writers either jot down their thoughts bit by bit, in short, sentences, which apparently mean much more than they say
>
> or
>
> they hold a deluge of words as though necessary to make the reader understand the deep meaning of their sentences

Some sentences need only a few deletions for clarification, but others require major recasting and additions; they must be read carefully and put into the reader's own words.

> Some in their discourse desire rather commendation of wit, in being able to hold all arguments, than of judgment, in discerning what is true; as if it were a praise to know what might be said, and not what should be thought.

After studying it, a reader might recast the sentence as follows:

> In conversation, some people desire praise for their abilities to maintain the conversation rather than for their abilities to identify what is true or false, as though it were better to sound good than to know what is truth or fiction.

2. Identifying the stated or implied meaning. *What is the author stating or suggesting?*

The literal meaning of a text does not always correspond with the intended meaning. To understand a passage fully, readers must determine which meaning—if there is more than one—is the intended meaning of the passage.

Consider the following sentence:

> If his notice was sought, an expression of courtesy and interest gleamed out upon his features; proving that there was light within him and that it was only the outward medium of the intellectual lamp that obstructed the rays in their passage.

Interpreted literally, this Nathaniel Hawthorne metaphor suggests that a light-generating lamp exists inside of the human body. Since this is impossible, the reader must look to the metaphoric meaning of the passage to properly understand it. In the metaphor, Hawthorne refers to the human mind—consciousness—as a lamp that emits light, and other people cannot always see the lamp because the outside "medium"—the human body—sometimes blocks it.

3.   Identifying the tone or mood of the selection. *What feeling does the text evoke?*

To answer these types of questions, readers must look closely at individual words and their connotations; for example, the words *stubborn* and *firm* have almost the same definition, but a writer who describes a character as *stubborn* rather than *firm* is probably suggesting something negative about the character.

Writing

The ACT writing exam allocates only thirty minutes to the composition of a well-organized, fully developed essay. Writing a satisfactory essay in this limited time requires the ability to quickly determine a thesis, organize ideas, and produce adequate examples to support the ideas.

An essay written in thirty minutes might not represent the best process writing—an ACT essay might lack the perfection and depth that weeks of proofreading and editing give to research papers. Process is undoubtedly important, but students must consider the time constraints of the ACT. Completion of the essay is just as important as organization, development, and language use.

The thesis, the organization of ideas, and the support make the framework of a good essay. Before the actual writing begins, a writer must create a mental outline by establishing a thesis, or main idea, and one or more specific supporting ideas (the number of ideas will depend on the length and content of the essay). Supporting ideas should not be overcomplicated; they are simply ideas that justify or explain the thesis. The writer must introduce and explain each supporting idea, and the resultant supporting paragraph should answer the *why?* or *who cares?* questions that the thesis may evoke.

Once the thesis and supporting ideas are identified, writers must determine the order in which the ideas will appear in the essay. A good introduction usually explains the thesis and briefly introduces the supporting ideas. Explanation of the supporting ideas should follow, with each idea in its own paragraph. The final paragraph, the conclusion, usually restates the thesis or summarizes the main ideas of the essay.

Adhering to this mental outline when the writing begins will help the writer organize and develop the essay. Using the Organization and Development scoring guides to evaluate practice essays will help to reinforce the process skills. The Word Choice and Sentence Formation scoring guides will help to strengthen language skills—the vital counterpart to essay organization and development.

Pronunciation Guide

a — track
ā — mate
ä — father
â — care
e — pet
ē — be
i — bit
ī — bite
o — job
ō — wrote
ô — port, horse, **fought**
ōō — proof
ŏŏ — book
u — pun
ū — you
û — purr
ə — about, system, supper, circus
îr — steer
ë — Fr. coeur
oi — toy

Word List

Lesson 1
abet
coerce
divulge
dogmatic
extraneous
gregarious
insipid
jaundiced
meticulous
temerity

Lesson 2
anathema
banter
castigate
docile
emaciated
gauche
heresy
ignominy
libation
motley

Lesson 3
avarice
bacchanalian
bastion
copious
extradite
furtive
irascible
jettison
mercenary
ostracize

Lesson 4
appease
argot
augment
bigot
candid
chaos
expunge
jingoism
negligence
strident

Lesson 5
adamant
clement
cliché
diffident
disparity
extol
inexorable
opus
ostensible
rancor

Lesson 6
apathy
condone
connoisseur
credence
cult
dilettante
enigma
jaunty
nuance
officious

Lesson 7
ambivalent
concur
culmination
cynical
demagogue
demure
destitute
dilemma
erudite
intrepid

Lesson 8
abate
abhor
austere
decorum
dole
droll
duplicity
effigy
extrovert
gamut

Lesson 9
collaborate
contrite
emulate
enhance
enunciate
evoke
expatriate
frowzy
heinous
impeccable
impound
inane
magnanimous
sere
unctuous

Lesson 10
acrimony
balk
cajole
dour
expound
exult
feasible
fiasco
fluctuate
harry
incognito
inscrutable
lethargy
métier
omniscient

Lesson 11
affable
agrarian
arduous
avid
dolorous
epistle
explicit
formidable
gadfly
gargantuan
grandiloquent
grimace
harangue
humility
sycophant

Lesson 12
altercation
audacity
evince
exhort
expedient
galvanize
hue
hyperbole
implacable
incarcerate
incisive
lexicon
ominous
pertinent
sanction

Lesson 13
acquit
adulation
barrister
bawdy
chastise
circumvent
clandestine
culinary
deprecate
frugal
inert
jocose
latent
myriad
pernicious

Lesson 14
amicable
bask
charlatan
enraptured
fickle
genial
hoax
juggernaut
levity
marital
mundane
naive
nocturnal
novice
obstreperous

Lesson 15
befuddle
chutzpah
complacent
connive
crass
fallacy
hypercritical
indiscreet
laudable
liege
noxious
odium
pandemonium
parsimonious
verbose

Lesson 16
linguistics
pique
plebeian
precocious
predatory
prowess
pugnacious
purloin
pusillanimous
quell
quixotic
rabble
rabid
raconteur
vindictive

Lesson 17
agnostic
caustic
circumspect
exodus
hurtle
penitent
raillery
renegade
retribution
scourge
taciturn
terse
uncanny
vindicate
zephyr

Lesson 18
discordant
expedite
filibuster
impregnable
inherent
invective
irreverent
pithy
pliable
pristine
prodigal
subjugate
tenuous
torpid
xenophobia

Lesson 19
approbation
arbiter
archetype
attrition
burgeon
commensurate
confluence
coup
epicurean
mellifluous
oeuvre
secular
vacuous
vagary
verdant

Lesson 20
accolade
demur
derivative
dissident
insouciant
invidious
limpid
petulant
proliferate
ruminate
static
stipulate
tenet
vigilant
zeitgeist

Lesson 21
albeit
ancillary
asinine
august
autodidact
behest
conduit
dossier
indefatigable
indiscretion
martyr
osmosis
philatelist
picayune
semblance

Book Two

Vocabulary
Power Plus
for the **ACT**
Vocabulary,
Reading, and Writing
Exercises for High Scores

Lesson One

1. **divulge** (di vulj´) v. to tell; to reveal (as a secret)
The reporter was fired when she *divulged* information from a classified document.
syn: unveil; disclose　　　　　　　　　　　　　*ant: conceal*

2. **abet** (ə bet´) v. to assist or encourage, especially in wrongdoing
Jim refused to *abet* the criminal's escape by hiding him in the basement.
syn: promote; incite　　　　　　　　　　　　　*ant: impede; dissuade*

3. **dogmatic** (dôg mat´ ik) adj. arrogant and stubborn about one's beliefs
Because of the professor's *dogmatic* approach, the students were afraid to ask questions.
syn: dictatorial　　　　　　　　　　　　　*ant: open-minded*

4. **insipid** (in sip´ id) adj. lacking flavor; dull; not at all stimulating
My mom wanted me to be an accountant, but I found the classes boring and *insipid*.
syn: flat; lifeless　　　　　　　　　　　　　*ant: challenging*

5. **extraneous** (ik strā´ nē əs) adj. not essential; not constituting a vital part
The professor felt that the *extraneous* paragraph in the essay detracted from the more important information.
syn: irrelevant; superfluous　　　　　　　　　　*ant: essential; critical*

6. **coerce** (kō ûrs´) v. to force by using pressure, intimidation, or threats
Jerry preferred basketball, but his father *coerced* him into playing football.
syn: compel

7. **jaundiced** (jôn´ dist) adj. prejudiced; hostile
Gabe had a *jaundiced* view of Iraq after losing his wife in the Gulf War.
syn: skeptical; cynical　　　　　　　　　　　　*ant: believing; trusting*

8. **meticulous** (mi tik´ yə ləs) adj. extremely, sometimes excessively, careful about small details; precise
With *meticulous* care, he crafted a miniature dollhouse for his daughter.
syn: fastidious　　　　　　　　　　　　　*ant: sloppy*

9. **temerity** (tə mer´ i tē) *n.* recklessness; a foolish disregard of danger
I couldn't believe that Bret had the *temerity* to bungee jump over a lake full of alligators.
syn: audacity   *ant: prudence*

10. **gregarious** (gri gâr´ ē əs) *adj.* sociable; fond of the company of others
Just before he was diagnosed with clinical depression, Raji went from being *gregarious* to being antisocial.
syn: genial; friendly   *ant: reclusive*

Exercise I

Words in Context

From the list below, supply the words needed to complete the paragraph. Some words will not be used.

divulge	abet	temerity	insipid	gregarious	coerce	jaundiced

A.   Jasmine had thought that her irresponsible days of _____ were far behind her until Kayla showed up at her door. After only three days of freedom from the county correctional facility, Kayla had begun her old scheming again. She went to the house to _____ Jasmine into helping her move a truckload of stolen goods to another state—an easy job, she claimed, and virtually no risk. It would even be fun, she claimed.

"Let me get this straight. You've been out of jail for three days, and you already want me to _____ you in your scheme to commit a crime? Are you crazy?"

Jasmine still had a(n) _____ attitude toward her sister because Kayla, prior to her first sentence, "borrowed" Jasmine's car for a robbery and nearly got Jasmine arrested as a result.

"Sorry, Kayla, but I'm quite happy with my _____, uneventful life. Please leave, and don't come back."

From the list below, supply the words needed to complete the paragraph. Some words will not be used.

dogmatic abet gregarious divulge extraneous coerce meticulous

B.   Mr. Knight learned the _____ art of watchmaking during a three-year stay in Switzerland more than forty years ago. Since that time, he has spent countless evenings in his basement workshop assembling the tiny, complex machines. As a[n] _____ grandfather, Mr. Knight often invites his grandchildren to his shop, where they watch with amazement through a large magnifying glass and see a newly assembled pocket watch tick for the first time.

"Watches are such perfect machines; there's no room for _____ parts or over-engineering. And then, to see such a tiny machine operate under its own power—it amazes me every time."

When asked about his thoughts on the mass production techniques of modern watches, Knight revealed his _____ belief that Old World skills made watches much more valuable.

"Oh, yes, the new watches are inexpensive and readily available, which fills the practical need, but they lack the sentiment and the many hours of craftsmanship that should go into a fine piece of jewelry."

"These watches," he says as he points to a sparkling display cabinet, "have character."

Mr. Knight hopes someday to _____ the many secrets of his trade to his youngest grandson, who can then carry on the family tradition for years to come.

Exercise II

Sentence Completion

Complete the sentence in a way that shows you understand the meaning of the italicized vocabulary word.

1. Rhea lacks *temerity*, so she definitely would not...

2. I've never been *gregarious*, so at parties I tend to...

3. Mel thinks musicals are *insipid*, so when I asked her to see *Miss Saigon* with me, she...

4. Hikers should avoid packing *extraneous* gear because...

5. A *jaundiced* judge might not be able to...

6. Lisa decided to *abet* the bank robber by...

7. Anna's *meticulous* cleaning habits ensure that her room is always...

8. I made my psychiatrist promise not to *divulge* any...

9. My *dogmatic* English teacher refused to...

10. My boss tried to *coerce* me into attending the company picnic by...

Exercise III

Roots, Prefixes, and Suffixes

Study the entries and answer the questions below.

The prefix *mal* means "bad" or "evil."
The root *bene* means "good."
The root *dict* means "to speak."
The root *vol* means "to wish."
The root *fact* means "making, doing"; *factor* means "one who does."

A. Using literal translations as guidance, define the following words without using a dictionary.

1. malevolent   4. benevolent
2. malediction   5. benediction
3. malefactor   6. benefactor

B. After a biopsy, tumors are generally labeled _____ or _____.

C. List as many other related words as you can that begin with either *mal* or *bene*.

Exercise IV

Inference

Complete the sentences by inferring information about the italicized word from its context.

A. If students complain about a teacher's *insipid* lectures, the teacher should...

B. Since dad had a handful of *extraneous* parts after assembling Kyle's bicycle, Kyle might...

C. Martin's refusal to *divulge* the location of the military base probably means that the base is...

Exercise V

Writing

Here is a writing prompt similar to the one you will find on the essay writing portion of the ACT.

> Eliminating the traditional failing letter grade of F has been a much discussed but rarely implemented idea. Citing the potential for psychological harm of students receiving failing grades, some opponents of the F want to replace the letter with an I for "incomplete," thus allowing students to finish courses well past the former grading deadlines. Opponents claim that eliminating failure, essentially, will fail to prepare students for real life, replete with real failure, or at least the possibility and likelihood of failure.
>
> Take a stand on the letter grade of F and write a letter to the school board. Be sure to support your argument with at least three detailed points.

Thesis: Write a *one-sentence* response to the above assignment. Make certain this single sentence offers a clear statement of your position.

Example: If inflating a letter grade can give students confidence to help them succeed, then it is a great idea.

_____

_____

Organizational Plan: List at least three subtopics you will use to support your main idea. This list is your outline.

1. _____

2. _____

3. _____

Draft: Following your outline, write a good first draft of your essay. Remember to support all your points with examples, facts, references to reading, etc.

Review and Revise: Exchange essays with a classmate. Using the scoring guide for Organization on page 224, score your partner's essay (while he or she scores yours). Focus on the organizational plan and use of language conventions. If necessary, rewrite your essay to improve the organizational plan and the use of language.

Exercise VI

English Practice

Identifying Sentence Errors

Identify the errors in the following sentences. Choose the answer that fixes the error. If the sentence contains no error, select NO CHANGE.

1. If the alarm had gone off earlier, more people <u>could of escaped</u> before the building collapsed.
   A. NO CHANGE
   B. could escape
   C. could have escaped
   D. would of escaped

2. The <u>principals of good sportsmanship</u> demand that we cheer the achievements of both teams.
   F. NO CHANGE
   G. principals of best sportsmanship
   H. principles of being good sports
   J. principles of good sportsmanship

3. Neither Kelley nor Larry <u>are planning</u> to attend the conference in November.
   A. NO CHANGE
   B. is planning
   C. is planned
   D. are planned

4. The boat sailed under the bridge and <u>was rocking from the waves</u>.
   F. NO CHANGE
   G. rocked from the waves
   H. was rocked by the waves
   J. rocked the waves

5. There were <u>less people</u> on that cruise than usual because of the weather.
   A. NO CHANGE
   B. fewer people
   C. less persons
   D. much less people

Improving Sentences

The underlined portion of each sentence below contains some flaw. Select the answer that best corrects the flaw.

6.   Lori said to her mother that she needed to buy some new clothes.
     F. said to her mother that Lori needed to buy some new clothes
     G. said that her mother needed to buy some new clothes
     H. said mom wanted to buy herself some new clothes
     J. said to her mother that, "She needs to buy some new clothes."

7.   Softened by the boiling water, Ramona mashed the potatoes.
     A. Softened by the boiling water Ramona mashed the potatoes.
     B. Ramona mashed the potatoes; they had been softened by the boiling water.
     C. Ramona mashed the potatoes that had been softened by the boiling water.
     D. Ramona mashed the potatoes by the boiling water.

8.   The founders of the United States selected the colors of the flag for their symbolism: white for the purity of the new nation's aspirations, red to stand for the blood shed gaining and keeping freedom, and blue for loyalty.
     F. red that stands for the blood
     G. red for the blood
     H. red, the color of blood
     J. red like the blood

9.   After several attempts to call, Doug still couldn't get through the line was always busy.
     A. get through, the line was
     B. get through although the line was
     C. get through, and the line was
     D. get through because the line was

10. Because she was on a diet every day, Naomi only ate three light meals.
     F. only Naomi ate three light meals
     G. Naomi ate only three light meals
     H. Naomi ate three light meals only
     J. three light meals were only eaten by Naomi

Vocabulary
Power Plus
for the ACT
Vocabulary,
Reading, and Writing
Exercises for High Scores

Lesson Two

1. **heresy** (her´ i sē) *n.* the crime of holding a belief that goes against established doctrine
During the Inquisition, those found guilty of *heresy* were sometimes burned at the stake.

   ant: orthodoxy

2. **docile** (dos´ əl) *adj.* easy to teach or manage; obedient
The poodle, usually *docile*, went mad and attacked its owner.
syn: submissive; compliant   *ant: unmanageable; willful*

3. **libation** (lī bā´ shən) *n.* a drink, especially an alcoholic one
When we visited the vineyard, we were offered a small *libation* at the end of our tour.
syn: intoxicant

4. **anathema** (ə nath´ ə mə) *n.* 1. a hated, repellant person or thing
1. Cannibalism is *anathema* to almost every society on the planet.
1. *syn: abhorration; detestation*   *ant: beloved*

5. **banter** (ban´ tər) *n.* teasing; playful conversation
At the reunion, Ruth enjoyed listening to the *banter* of her husband and his old college roommate.
syn: joshing; badinage; raillery   *ant: vituperation*

6. **castigate** (kas´ ti gāt) *v.* to criticize or punish severely
The parson *castigated* the boy for noisily chewing gum in church.
syn: reprimand; chastise; scold   *ant: praise*

7. **gauche** (gōsh) *adj.* lacking social graces; tactless
Some people use a fork to eat pizza because they think it is *gauche* to use their fingers.
syn: awkward   *ant: graceful*

8. **ignominy** (ig´ nə min ē) *n.* public shame, disgrace, or dishonor
The mayor fell from public acclaim to complete *ignominy* in a week when her cocaine habit was discovered.
syn: disgrace; infamy   *ant: renown; eminence; repute*

9. **motley** (mot´ lē) *adj.* made up of dissimilar parts; being of many colors
The international clown convention was a *motley* sight in the otherwise dull exhibition center.
syn: varied   *ant: uniform; homogeneous; similar*

10. **emaciated** (i mā´ shē āt ed) *adj.* extremely thin; wasted away
Dead from starvation, the *emaciated* prisoner was buried in the camp cemetery.
syn: withered   *ant: plump; fattened*

Exercise I

Words in Context

From the list below, supply the words needed to complete the paragraph. Some words will not be used.

gauche   castigate   heresy   banter   anathema   ignominy   emaciated

A.   After five years of starvation and torture, the _____ Kwame prayed for death. Hope was a foreign concept to him now; he no longer remembered what it was like to live in the sunlight. When he tried to remember, all he could visualize were the three years of humiliating _____ that preceded his incarceration. He couldn't even remember the faces of his wife and children anymore.
    The whole thing began when Kwame's brother, a schoolteacher, wrote a letter to a nonprofit agency in the United States to appeal for educational funds. The letter was intercepted, and Sirajul's agents brought the letter to Sirajul himself. The mad dictator declared that any letter that portrayed his reign in a bad light was total _____. Kwame's brother was executed, and then, to make a point, Sirajul _____ then, imprisoned the entire family. While dictators like Sirajul were a[n] _____ to virtually anyone in the civilized world, few people had the means to stop them.

From the list below, supply the words needed to complete the paragraph. Some words will not be used.

gauche   motley   emaciated   libation   banter   docile   heresy

B.   The actors gathered in the banquet room after the closing night of the hit play. Sounds of lighthearted _____ filled the room; some of the more _____ performers thought nothing of picking two or more cold _____ at a time from the trays of the servers. The players were still in costumes depicting various cultures and historic eras, and arriving guests paused at the door to take in the _____ sight. The company had just completed its twentieth and final show of a successful run, and the performers were happy to relax. The spirited staff, laughing and carousing, became _____ only when the director raised her hands to quiet the room. Anticipating her words of encouragement, none of the actors suspected that she was about to announce her retirement.

Exercise II

Words in Context

Complete the sentence in a way that shows you understand the meaning of the italicized vocabulary word.

1.   If Sarita tells me that her new dress is *motley*, I can assume that it is...

2.   The *emaciated* girl looked as if she had not...

3.   The Spanish Inquisition charged don Torino with *heresy* for allegedly...

4.   A traditional *libation* at weddings and New Year's Eve parties is...

5.   A supervisor might *castigate* an employee if...

6.   When the teacher returned to find a *docile* class, he knew that...

7.   At a wedding, it might be considered *gauche* if you...

8.   One thing that is *anathema* to our society is...

9. The television evangelist faced *ignominy* when the public…

10. If someone you have a crush on engages in extended *banter* with you, you might conclude…

Exercise III

Roots, Prefixes, and Suffixes

Study the entries and answer the questions that follow.

The root *anthro* means "man."
The suffix *ology* means "study of."
The root *theo* means "god" or "religion."
The suffix *oid* means "having the shape of."
The root *morph* means "shape."
The prefix *a* means "not."
The suffix *cracy* means "government by."

A. Using literal translations as guidance, define the following words without using a dictionary.

1. anthropology
2. theology
3. anthropoid

4. anthropomorphic
5. atheism
6. theocracy

B. What is studied in the science of sociology?

C. List as many words as you can think of that contain either *anthro* or *theo* or end in *ology*.

Exercise IV

Inference

Complete the sentences by inferring information about the italicized word from its context.

A. When offered food for the first time in weeks, the *emaciated* castaway probably…

B.   If Grace complained that Jeremy was *gauche* on the dance floor, you
     might assume that Jeremy was...

C.   A *docile* dog is probably easier to train than an aggressive dog because...

Exercise V

Critical Reading

*Below is a reading passage followed by several multiple-choice questions similar to
the ones you will encounter on the ACT. Carefully read the passage and choose the
best answer to each of the questions.*

H. G. Wells, author of *The Invisible Man* and *The Time Machine*, was also very
interested in history. The following passage, "Primitive Thought," is adapted
from Wells's *A Short History of the World*. In it, Wells speculates on the origins
of human thought and religion.

　　　How did it feel to be alive in the early days of the human adventure? How did
men and women think and what did they think in those remote days four hundred
centuries ago? Those were days long before the written record of any human
impressions, and we are left almost entirely to inference and guesswork in our
5　answers to these questions.
　　　Primitive humans probably thought very much as a child thinks. They conjured
up images or images presented themselves to their minds, and they acted in
accordance with the emotions these pictures aroused. So a child or an uneducated
person does today. Systematic thinking is apparently a comparatively late
10　development in human experience; it has not played any great part in human life
until within the last three thousand years. And even today those who really control
and order their thoughts are a small minority of humankind. Most of the world still
lives by imagination and passion.
　　　Probably the earliest human societies were small family groups. Just as the
15　flocks and herds of the earlier mammals arose out of families which remained
together and multiplied, so probably did the earliest human tribes. But before this
could happen, a certain restraint upon the primitive egotisms of the individual
had to be established. The fear of the father and respect for the mother had to be
extended into adult life, and the natural jealousy of the old man of the group for
20　the younger males as they grew up had to be mitigated. Human social life grew up
out of the reaction between the instinct of the young to go off by themselves as they
grew up, on the one hand, and the dangers and disadvantages of separation on the
other.
　　　Some writers would have us believe that respect and fear of the Old Man and
25　the emotional reaction of the primitive to older protective women, exaggerated
in dreams and enriched by imagination, played a large part in the beginnings of
primitive religion and in the conception of gods and goddesses. Associated with
this respect for powerful or helpful personalities was a dread and exaltation of such

personages after their deaths, due to their reappearance in dreams. It was easy to
30　believe they were not truly dead but only fantastically transferred to a remoteness
of greater power.

The dreams, imaginations, and fears of a child are far more vivid and real
than those of a modern adult, and primitive humans were always somewhat like
children. They were nearer to the animals also, and could suppose these animals
35　to have motives and reactions like their own. They could imagine animal helpers,
animal enemies, animal gods. One needs only to have been an imaginative child
oneself to realize again how important, significant, portentous or kind strangely
shaped rocks, lumps of wood, exceptional trees, or the like may have appeared to
the men of the Old Stone Age; and how dream and fancy would create stories and
40　legends about such things that would become credible as they were told. Some of
these stories would be good enough to remember and tell again. The women would
tell them to the children and so establish a tradition. To this day most imaginative
children invent stories in which some favourite doll or animal or some fantastic
being figures as the hero, and primitive storytellers probably did the same—with a
45　much stronger disposition to believe his hero real.

At the same time, primitive humans were not very critical in their associations of
cause with effect; they very easily connected an effect with something quite wrong
as its cause. "You do so and so," they said, "and so and so happens." You give a
child a poisonous berry and it dies. You eat the heart of a valiant enemy and you
50　become strong. There we have two bits of cause and effect association, one true one
false. We call the system of cause and effect in the mind of a primitive, Fetish; but
Fetish is simply primitive science. It differs from modern science in that it is totally
unsystematic and uncritical and so more frequently wrong.

In many cases other erroneous ideas were soon corrected by experience; but
55　there was a large series of issues of very great importance to primitive humans,
where they sought persistently for causes and found explanations that were wrong
but not sufficiently wrong nor so obviously wrong as to be detected. It was a
matter of great importance to them that game should be abundant or fish plentiful
and easily caught, and no doubt they tried and believed in a thousand charms,
60　incantations and omens to determine these desirable results. Another great concern
of his was illness and death. Occasionally infections crept through the land and
people died of them. Occasionally people were stricken by illness and died or
were enfeebled without any manifest cause. This too must have given the hasty,
emotional primitive mind much feverish exercise. Dreams and fantastic guesses
65　made primitive people blame this, or appeal for help to that person, or beast, or
thing.

Quite early in the little human tribe, older, steadier minds who shared the fears
and the imaginations, but who were a little more forceful than the others must
have asserted themselves, to advise, to prescribe, to command. This they declared
70　unlucky and that imperative; this an omen of good and that an omen of evil. The
expert in Fetish, the Medicine Man, was the first priest. He exhorted, he interpreted
dreams, he warned, he performed the complicated hocus pocus that brought luck or
averted calamity. Primitive religion was not so much what we now call religion as
practice and observance, and the early priest dictated what was indeed an arbitrary
75　primitive practical science.

1. According to lines 6-13, people who think systematically
   A. determine the course of human progression.
   B. are outnumbered by people driven by emotion.
   C. composed a large portion of early civilization.
   D. are the modern equivalent of medicine men.

2. The overall tone of this passage is
   F. simplistic and speculative.
   G. scholarly and authoritative.
   H. facetious and entertaining.
   J. strident and conciliatory.

3. As used in the passage, the word *egotisms* (line 17) most nearly means
   A. vanity.
   B. self-consciousness.
   C. conceit.
   D. self-centeredness.

4. Which choice best states the psychological conflict that guided human social interaction?
   F. fear of father versus respect for mother
   G. dangers of separation versus desire to be independent
   H. instinct to be independent versus jealousy of larger families
   J. desires to remain together versus respect for father

5. As used in line 39, the word *fancy* most nearly means
   A. elegant.
   B. imagination.
   C. fond.
   D. anxious.

6. Which of the following is the best paraphrase of the sentence "Fetish is simply primitive science" (line 52)?
   F. Science is not based on superstition.
   G. The original word for science was fetish.
   H. The roots of modern science lie in superstition.
   J. Fetish and superstition are primitive.

7. According to the last paragraph, how did primitive Medicine Men attain their status?
   A. They demonstrated more knowledge and power than others in their tribe did.
   B. They rose in status by asserting their charismatic personalities.
   C. The oldest man in the tribe was chosen as Medicine Man.
   D. The Medicine Man was revealed in a tribal dream.

8. According to the passage, which of the following is *not* a step in the development of primitive science and religion?
   F. Primitive people observed events and their apparent causes.
   G. Primitive people attempted to find the means to control the forces that affected their lives.
   H. Primitive people attributed power to other people, animals, and objects.
   J. Primitive people elected a priest from among their tribal members.

9. According to this passage, primitive religion was the precursor to
   A. superstition.
   B. practical science.
   C. respect for elders.
   D. a rapid increase in population.

10. This passage would most likely be found in
    F. a popular science magazine.
    G. an introductory history book.
    H. an encyclopedia of world religion.
    J. a book of ancient mythology.

Lesson Three

1. **avarice** (av´ ə ris) *n.* greed; desire for wealth
   He became a doctor, not to save lives but to appease his *avarice*.
   syn: acquisitiveness   *ant: largesse*

2. **furtive** (fûr´ tiv) *adj.* stealthy; secretive
   Not wanting to be rude, Jean cast only a *furtive* glance at the man's prominent scar.
   syn: surreptitious; sneaky   *ant: overt*

3. **bacchanalian** (bak ə nāl´ yən) *adj.* wild and drunken
   Adam paid for his *bacchanalian* weekend when he flunked the exam on Monday.
         ant: restrained

4. **extradite** (ek´ strə dīt) *v.* to turn over or deliver to the legal jurisdiction of another government or authority
   After two months of incarceration in Sacramento, the suspect was *extradited* to Florida.
   syn: deport

5. **copious** (kō´ pē əs) *adj.* numerous; large in quantity
   It is good to drink a *copious* amount of water before and after working out.
   syn: profuse; abundant   *ant: sparse*

6. **irascible** (i ras´ ə bəl) *adj.* easily angered
   We walk on eggshells around Marty because he is so *irascible*.
   syn: irritable; ill-tempered   *ant: easygoing*

7. **mercenary** (mûr´ sə ner ē) *n.* a professional soldier hired by a foreign army
   Though American by birth, the *mercenary* fought for France.
         ant: volunteer

8. **bastion** (bas´ chən) *n.* a strong defense or fort (or something likened to it)
   The United States has been called the *bastion* of democracy.
   syn: stronghold

9. **jettison** (jet´ i sən) *v.* to cast overboard; to discard
The passengers quickly *jettisoned* the heavy cargo from the damaged plane.
syn: deploy; throw away   *ant: retain*

10. **ostracize** (os´ trə sīz) *v.* to banish; to shut out from a group or society by common consent
The strict religious community *ostracized* Eli when he married a woman of another faith.
syn: exile   *ant: accept*

Exercise I

Words in Context

From the list below, supply the words needed to complete the paragraph. Some words will not be used.

extradite	ostracize	furtive	avarice
mercenary	bacchanalian	bastion	copious

A.   Hired to combat an increase in drug trafficking, the _____ silently crawled through the fence line of the kingpin's plantation and found a good hiding place. For two days, Manco sat in the patch and observed the mansion—supposedly an impenetrable _____ from which the criminal operated his international cartel. Manco was relieved to see that the rumors were false; the kingpin's _____ lifestyle of nightly parties would make Manco's job simple because of the _____ noise and inadequate light beyond the cocktail area. After a[n] _____ infiltration of the mansion, Manco would have an easy time arresting the man, handcuffing him, sneaking him out, and then _____ him to the States, where he would face trial on a number of charges. The drug lord was about to become a victim of his own _____—had he kept his illegal business small and untraceable, no one would have hired Manco to deal with him.

From the list below, supply the words needed to complete the paragraph. Some words will not be used.

bastion   jettison   irascible   avarice   ostracize

B.   Isabel's _____ personality had gotten her into trouble before, but never as it did now. In reaction to her outburst during the assembly, Isabel's class _____ her. Classmates would not sit next to Isabel, let alone speak to her. If her disruption had happened on a ship, Isabel thought, the passengers might have _____ her over the side.

Exercise II

Sentence Completion

Complete the sentence in a way that shows you understand the meaning of the italicized vocabulary word.

1.   A criminal might be *extradited* to her home state for…

2.   After a *bacchanalian* weekend, Ethan felt…

3.   It is a burden to have an *irascible* supervisor because…

4.   The *mercenary* received no payment and refused to…

5.   The failing company had to *jettison* its…

6.   The cliquish teens *ostracized* Raymond from their group because…

7.   If I allow *avarice* to guide my career, I might choose to…

8.   There was *copious* weeping whenever…

9.   A church might be called a *bastion* of…

10. One might want to be especially *furtive* when…

Roots, Prefixes, and Suffixes

Study the entries and answer the questions that follow.

The root *aud* means "hear."
The root *herb* means "grass, weed."
The roots *cis* and *cide* mean "cut" or "kill."
The roots *vis* and *vid* mean "see."
The suffixes *ible* and *able* mean "able."
The prefix *in* means "into."

A. *Using literal translations as guidance, define the following words without using a dictionary:*

    1. audible   4. vista
    2. visionary   5. auditory
    3. herbicide   6. incision

B. The root *sui* in the word "suicide" probably means _____.

C. List as many words as you can that have the roots *aud* and *vid* in them.

D. Write one example of an *incisive* comment.

E. List as many words as you can that end in *cide*.

Inference

Complete the sentences by inferring information about the italicized word from its context.

A. If the king's *avarice* gets out of control, he might decide to…

B. Even a little good-humored teasing might cause the *irascible* Cary to…

C. If his promised wages do not arrive before the battle, the *mercenary* will probably…

Exercise V

Writing

Here is a writing prompt similar to the one you will find on the essay writing portion of the ACT.

Imagine routinely diving for cover beneath your desk as practice for surviving a nuclear bomb. This was a reality for students in the United States and the Soviet Union during the height of the Cold War, prior to the fall of the Berlin Wall in 1989 and the subsequent collapse of the Soviet Union.

History attributes fifty years of peace to the Cold War: Two superpowers having the ability to annihilate each other prevented either side from starting a war. Many historians, therefore, ascribe to the maxim that applies to smaller segments of "an armed society is a polite society."

Based on your knowledge and belief of human nature, is the Cold War scenario a truism that applies to all people and all civilization? Will one nation, or person, naturally attempt to conquer the other simply because it has the means to conquer and cannot be stopped?

Base your argument on a situation in your own life, an example from world history, or an imagined scenario that resembles the situation of the Cold War, wherein the only thing preventing two people, or nations, from attacking one another is the fact that one would destroy the other in kind.

Thesis: Write a *one-sentence* response to the above assignment. Make certain this single sentence offers a clear statement of your position.

Example: If there is one constant in the history of humanity, it is that the stronger nation will influence, invade, or conquer the weaker nation.

_____

_____

Organizational Plan: List at least three subtopics you will use to support your main idea. This list is your outline.

1. _____

2. _____

3. _____

Draft: Following your outline, write a good first draft of your essay. Remember to support all your points with examples, facts, references to reading, etc.

Review and Revise: Exchange essays with a classmate. Using the scoring guide for Development of Ideas on page 225, score your partner's essay (while he or she scores yours). Focus on the development of ideas and use of language conventions. If necessary, rewrite your essay to incorporate more (or more relevant) support, and to improve your use of language.

Exercise VI

English Practice

Improving Paragraphs
Read the following passage and then choose the best revision for the underlined portions of the paragraph. The questions will require you to make decisions regarding the revision of the reading selection. Some revisions are not of actual mistakes, but will improve the clarity of the writing.

[1]

A book is now a common object, yet there was a time when the book was a rare and precious possession—a religious relic not available to the common person.

[2]

The earliest collections that we would recognize as "books" <u>was</u>[1] elaborate manuscripts produced in European monasteries. To ensure that ancient knowledge would not be lost, <u>monks made copies</u>[2] of the books they protected. The books produced during this period were exquisitely and elaborately illustrated with beautiful lettering called <u>calligraphy and fantastic images of snakes,</u>[3] demons, and mythological creatures.

1. A. NO CHANGE
   B. used to be
   C. wasn't
   D. were

2. F. NO CHANGE
   G. monk's copies
   H. copies were made by monks
   J. monks made a copy

3. A. NO CHANGE
   B. calligraphy, and fantastic snake images
   C. calligraphy including fantastic images of snakes
   D. calligraphy and fantastic snakes

[3]

The most important thing about these manuscripts is that they were considered sacred objects. The monks who sat for years working on single chapters of the Bible were not reproducing books—they were making the word of God available to the world.

[4]

Eventually, the production of books moved from the Church to the University, and books began to lose some of their religious emphasis. University student's[4] did not have access to the books locked away in monasteries. Also, they needed access to new kinds of non-religious books that were not easily available, even in the libraries of monasteries.

4. F. NO CHANGE
   G. student
   H. students
   J. students'

[5]

Two new kinds of institutions grew up around the universities to fulfill the demand: stationers,[5] and book copiers. These people provided paper and libraries of text books when a student needed[6] a text for a class, he would go to the stationers and copy it—by hand. The student could also pay a book copier to copy the book for himself.[7]

5. A. NO CHANGE
   B. stationers
   C. stationers:
   D. stationers'

6. F. NO CHANGE
   G. paper and libraries of text
      books. When a student
      needed
   H. paper and libraries of text
      books whenever a student
      needed
   J. paper and libraries of text
      books: When students
      needed

7. A. NO CHANGE
   B. his own
   C. both of them
   D. him

[6]

Then the whole book-producing industry began to change with the arrival of the printing press.[8] The printing press was not a single invention. It was the clever combination of many technologies that had been known for centuries.

8. Which revision of the first sentence offers a better transition between the two paragraphs?
   F. Next, the whole book-producing industry began to change.
   G. Omit "then"
   H. The tedium of hand-copying books was soon alleviated by the arrival of the printing press.
   J. Place a semicolon at the after the word press

[7]

The other inventions brought together to create the printing press were machines used for hundreds of years in Europe and Asia to press oil from olives and make wine from grapes; block[9] printing, which had been known in Europe since the return of Marco Polo from Asia.

9. A. NO CHANGE
   B. grapes; and
   C. grapes; and additionally,
   D. grapes, plus block

[8]

Olive oil was a valuable commodity of the ancient world, used as medicine, food, and fuel. Olive trees are very hardy, able to survive droughts and salty environments. The oil itself can last for many months—even years—without spoiling if stored in proper conditions.

10. Paragraph 8 should be
    F. moved to precede paragraph 2.
    G. moved to the end of the passage.
    H. revised to include more information on the medicinal value of olive oil.
    J. deleted from the passage.

[9]

The development of print technology created a need for other developments. Medieval manuscripts had been copied on vellum pages—a material made largely from linen. It was beautiful and durable, but far too expensive for the mass production of books. Likewise, the ink that had been used by the monks and later by university students and book copiers was expensive. Oil-based ink needed to be developed, as well as a paper that could be mass-produced inexpensively, yet still be durable enough to print a book that would last.

[10]

Ironically, the first books printed were Bibles and religious texts; so, while the printing press may have made books more available, it did not necessarily affect the subject matter of books.

[11]

However, by the 16th and 17th Century,[11] the Roman Catholic Church was losing much of its influence. Latin had been the primary language for the worship of God and for the exchange of intellectual ideas, but this was changing with the Protestant Reformation.[12] More people were learning to read, and they wanted to read things in they're own language.

11.A. NO CHANGE
   B. However by the 16th or 17th Century,
   C. However, by the 16th or 17th century,
   D. However by the sixteenth or seventeenth centuries

12.F. NO CHANGE
   G. Latin had been the primary language for the worship of God; and for the exchange of intellectual ideas. But this was changing with the Protestant Reformation.
   H. Latin has been the primary language for the worship of God and for the exchange of intellectual ideas, but this was changing with the Protestant Reformation.
   J. Latin has been the primary language for the worship of God and for the exchange of intellectual ideas, but this would soon be changed with the Protestant Reformation.

[12]

In addition, world exploration and the European colonization of Africa and the New World made people curious about faraway places. Writers and printers were only too happy to fill this demand for reading material for the curious middle classes. The modern book was born.

[13]

Long and interesting, every book, regardless of subject, has an ancestry that dates back to the monks in their medieval monasteries.[13] Were it not for such different endeavors as wine-making and world travel, the book as we know it might never have been developed.

13. A. NO CHANGE
   B. Every book, regardless of subject, has an ancestry that dates back to the monks in their medieval monasteries, long and interesting.
   C. Every book, regardless of subject, has a long and interesting ancestry that dates back to the monks in their medieval monasteries.
   D. Long and interesting, every book has an ancestry that dates to the medieval monks in monasteries.

14. Which two paragraphs could be combined to make the passage easier to read?
   F. Paragraphs 5 and 6
   G. Paragraphs 7 and 9
   H. Paragraphs 7 and 8
   J. Paragraphs 11 and 13

15. If the passage had to be shortened, which two paragraphs could be eliminated without changing the intent of the passage?
   A. Paragraphs 1 and 2
   B. Paragraphs 4 and 5
   C. Paragraph 6
   D. Paragraphs 10 and 11

Vocabulary
Power Plus
for the
ACT
Vocabulary,
Reading, and Writing
Exercises for High Scores

Lesson Four

1. **bigot** (big´ ət) *n.* one who is intolerant of differences in others
The *bigot* refused to share a cab with anyone of a different race.
syn: racist; extremist

2. **expunge** (ik spunj´) *v.* to erase or eliminate
If Moni can stay out of trouble for one year, her criminal record will be
expunged.
syn: obliterate   *ant: add*

3. **candid** (kan´ did) *adj.* outspoken; blunt
He gave a *candid* speech about the time he had spent in prison.
syn: frank; direct   *ant: evasive*

4. **argot** (är´ gət) *n.* special words or phrases used by a specific group of
    people
Don't agree to "a trip to the East River" proposed by anyone speaking Mafia
argot.
syn: jargon

5. **negligence** (neg´ li jəns) *n.* careless neglect, often resulting in injury
Sara's *negligence* allowed her toddler to fall from the hotel balcony.
syn: carelessness   *ant: care; attention*

6. **appease** (ə pēz´) *v.* to calm; to make satisfied (often only temporarily)
The small snack before dinner did nothing to *appease* Shane's appetite.
syn: mollify   *ant: aggravate*

7. **strident** (strīd´ nt) *adj.* harsh sounding; grating
Lisa's *strident* voice gave us all headaches.
syn: shrill   *ant: soothing*

8. **chaos** (kā´ os) *n.* complete disorder
The new teacher was expected to end the *chaos* and restore order in the
classroom.
syn: confusion; jumble   *ant: order; harmony*

9. **augment** (ôg ment´) *v.* to enlarge; to increase in amount or intensity
   I had to take a second job to *augment* my income after buying the new SUV.
   syn: expand; supplement   *ant: narrow; reduce*

10. **jingoism** (jing´ gō iz əm) *n.* extreme, chauvinistic patriotism, often favoring an aggressive, warlike foreign policy
    Because of his *jingoism*, the candidate lost the support of voters.

Exercise I

Words in Context

From the list below, supply the words needed to complete the paragraph. Some words will not be used.

augment   jingoism   argot   candid   chaos   appease

A.   The Prime Minister faced a tough decision in order to _____ an angered nation. The _____ resulting from the surprise attack fueled widespread _____, and citizens were tired of the administration's inaction. When he finally spoke, the Prime Minister delivered a[n] _____ address that revealed both his anger and his plan of counterattack.

From the list below, supply the words needed to complete the paragraph. Some words will not be used.

negligence	**augment**	**expunge**	**bigot**
argot	**strident**	**chaos**	**tradition**

B.   The ridiculous arguments of the outspoken _____ became too much for his opponents in the general population. When the man began to use the _____ of the despised slave trade to encourage his followers and _____ his arguments, many college-age protesters began to attend his rallies. Their _____ voices condemned not only the speaker, but also the _____ of the government in allowing his presence at state-funded institutions. The mainstream students wished that his views could be _____ from society.

Exercise II

Sentence Completion

Complete the sentence in a way that shows you understand the meaning of the italicized vocabulary word.

1. Theresa was *candid* about my new haircut; she told me that...

2. When I babysat the Patelli twins, my *negligence* led to...

3. I thought it was fair to accuse George of *jingoism* after he...

4. If I wanted to *augment* my savings account, I might...

5. The *argot* of pirates might include terms such as...

6. I realized my grandfather was a *bigot* when he told me...

7. One way to *appease* a crying child is...

8. My brother's voice becomes *strident* when he...

9. The atmosphere on the commuter train became one of *chaos* when...

10. My math teacher said he would *expunge* the "F" from my record if I...

Exercise III

Roots, Prefixes, and Suffixes

Study the entries and answer the questions that follow.

The root *alter* means "change" or "other."
The root *ego* means "self."
The root *mega* means "large."
The root *polis* means "city" or "state."
The root *centris* means "centered on."

A. *Using literal translations as guidance, define the following words without using a dictionary:*

1. megalopolis   4. metropolitan
2. alteration   5. egotist
3. alter ego   6. egocentric

B. A person who is a megalomaniac might not feel right unless

_____.

C. If you alter your plans, you _____.

D. List as many words as you can think of that begin with the root *ego*, and then do the same for the root *mega*.

Exercise IV

Inference

Complete the sentences by inferring information about the italicized word from its context.

A. The writer took offense at Marty's *candid* review because it...

B. When *negligence* becomes the main reason for damaged goods and low profits, the plant managers will probably...

C. If Colleen made *strident* sounds while practicing her saxophone, her parents probably...

Exercise V

Critical Reading

Below is a passage followed by several multiple-choice questions similar to the ones you will encounter on the ACT. Carefully read the passages and choose the best answer to each of the questions.

The Commonwealth of Pennsylvania is a wealth of natural resources, and the bounty has been claimed and reclaimed. The vast native forests and rich coal deposits built countless railroads and boroughs dotting the valleys of the Keystone State. There has been a price for the commodities. Timbering wiped

5   out Pennsylvania hardwood forests when loggers clamored for the massive white pines—the preferred lumber a century ago. Dozens of spent mines, years after their usefulness, leaked iron ore into creeks, making the water inhabitable to native trout for decades. Whitetail deer were hunted to virtual extinction by 1900. Nature is slow to recover, but after dozens of years, extensive legislation, and millions of

10   dollars in reclamation funds, the forests have since grown back and streams and forests teem with trout and deer. Now the allure of natural gas has again forced many residents to weigh the risks of extracting the prize from the earth. Every prize comes with risk, and sometimes the risk is that of losing the treasure itself. Consider the lessons learned in the mining town of Centralia.

15   All the small towns in the coal-rich hills of Central Pennsylvania look pretty much alike, except for Centralia. With a population of 10, Centralia is a twenty-first century ghost town. Sulfurous smoke vents through cracks in empty, overgrown streets and houses have collapsed into sink holes caused by mine subsidence. On April 1, 1996—April Fools' Day—the United States Supreme Court denied an

20   appeal of the 46 remaining residents of Centralia, Pennsylvania, who had filed preliminary legal objections to the condemnation of their homes. With this denial, these hapless citizens essentially lost the right to their homes.

Residents who chose to stay beyond the December 31, 1997, relocation deadline would forfeit the right to compensation from any federal or state agency or any

25   private enterprise for losses suffered, including loss of life.

The issue at hand was a 34-year-old mine fire burning beneath the homes, businesses, and streets of Centralia. What seemed to be an unfortunate accident in May of 1962 now appears to some to be a conspiracy on the part of the United States government to seize the rich coal

30   deposits that lie beneath the town and surrounding areas.

Proponents of the conspiracy theory cite a list of facts to substantiate the theory. Supposedly, holes in the strip mine that allowed the fire to travel beneath the surface had been sealed before the site was approved for use as a landfill. The PA government inspected and certified the site as safe to use; however, a few days

35   after the 1962 fire, firefighters found a hole that had been left open. In addition, the Department of Natural Resources drilled boreholes to monitor the underground fire—boreholes which subsequently provided more oxygen that helped the fire to spread.

What seemed to be half-hearted attempts to extinguish the fire fostered further
40 suspicion from conspiracy theorists. Only one serious attempt to control the burn
occurred in 1968 over a holiday weekend. Firefighters dug a trench to halt the
spread of the fire; however, crews worked only one daily shift, rather than the
24-hour shifts necessary to contain the fire. Crews even stopped for the holiday;
by the time they returned, the fire had spread beyond the trench. Neither did
45 the federal government prove very useful other than in purchasing the homes
in Centralia and relocating the residents. The Commonwealth of Pennsylvania
condemned the properties of the remaining residents in 1992, but failed to help
bring legal action to protect the rights and homes of the former Centralia residents.
In 1996, the Supreme Court denied any possibility of legal action on the part of the
50 residents and the Commonwealth of Pennsylvania.

Many remaining and former residents assert that when the final person leaves
Centralia, the land and the coal will become the property of the United States
government. They suspect that when the government owns the land, the means of
extinguishing the decades-old fire will be discovered, and the coal will be mined.
55 Is Centralia's plight the product of a government conspiracy or is it simply a
tragic accident? Perhaps only the future will tell, but for those whose entire family
histories have been lost, it's been a sad story that hasn't yet ended.

1. The passage suggests that the fire could have been stopped if
    A. the government had sent more firefighters.
    B. there had been a real fire to begin with.
    C. the firemen had worked more diligently.
    D. the homes in Centralia had been more valuable.

2. If the conspiracy theory is correct, what does the government stand to gain?
    F. the proceeds from mining coal on government land
    G. natural gas from the shale deposits around Centralia
    H. the data from long-term covert medical experiments
    J. a reason to use eminent domain to build a highway

3. According to the passage, how did the fire begin?
    A. Residents allowed a summer bonfire to get out of control.
    B. Garbage burning in a landfill started the fire.
    C. The fire began spontaneously in a bin full of oily rags.
    D. The passage does not include that information.

4. The author suggests that the Centralia fire is
    F. simply one event in a long series of mishaps in the process of extracting natural resources.
    G. merely a pretense to drill boreholes into the rich coal deposits.
    H. an event so unique that the town of Centralia has become famous as a result.
    J. a result of the decreased timber and wildlife after a century of exploitation.

5. Which of the following items is not required for limiting damage or repairing damage to natural resources?
    A. plenty of time for nature to recover
    B. help from the government
    C. large amounts of money
    D. laws governing the extraction of resources

6. What idea does the author of the passage hope to establish in lines 15-17?
    F. Life was difficult in Centralia, Pennsylvania, even before the fire.
    G. Prior to the fire, Centralia, Pennsylvania, was a thriving metropolis.
    H. Centralia, Pennsylvania, was a typical small town before the fire.
    J. Centralia, Pennsylvania, was an inappropriate place for a landfill.

7. As used in its context in line 18, the word *subsidence* most nearly means
    A. relocation.
    B. condemning.
    C. replenishment.
    D. erosion.

8. The method used initially to fight the fire was
    F. cutting the fire off from fuel.
    G. water immersion.
    H. carbon dioxide.
    J. burning the coal from two sides.

9. Which of the following is *not* a factor in the suspected conspiracy?
    A. The Commonwealth of Pennsylvania inspected the strip mine and certified it for use as a landfill.
    B. Boreholes drilled by the Department of Natural Resources may have provided oxygen and allowed the fire to spread.
    C. Residents of Centralia have been denied legal appeals to the condemnation of their homes.
    D. The Supreme Court denial was handed down on April Fool's Day.

10. What does the author conclude about the likelihood that the Centralia mine fire is a government conspiracy?
  - F. The author comes to no absolute conclusion, citing only what residents claim.
  - G. The author sums up the facts of the case and suggests that a conspiracy is possible.
  - H. The author sums up the facts of the case and suggests that a conspiracy is not likely.
  - J. The author offers no conclusion regarding the conspiracy, but expresses sympathy for the affected residents.

Book Two

Vocabulary
Power Plus
for the
ACT
Vocabulary,
Reading, and Writing
Exercises for High Scores

Lesson Five

1. **rancor** (rang´ kər) *n.* extreme hatred or ill will
   Whelan's double-dealing had Jack seething; he had never before felt so
   much *rancor* toward a lawyer.
   syn: animosity; enmity   *ant: amity; sympathy*

2. **inexorable** (in ek´ sər ə bal) *adj.* unrelenting; unavoidable
   Decades of harsh weather caused the *inexorable* erosion of the tombstone.
   syn: relentless; certain   *ant: avoidable; preventable*

3. **extol** (ik stōl´) *v.* to praise highly
   Emily *extolled* the virtues of her personal hero and mentor.
   syn: exalt; laud   *ant: chastise*

4. **clement** (klem´ ənt) *adj.* merciful; lenient
   Despite the abhorrent nature of the crime, the judge handed down a
   surprisingly *clement* sentence.
   syn: forbearing; benign   *ant: malevolent; harsh*

5. **cliché** (klē shā´) *n.* a worn-out idea or overused expression
   The candidate promised new ideas, but spouted only old *clichés* about
   government after her election.
   syn: platitude; banality

6. **adamant** (ad´ ə mant) *adj.* unyielding; firm in opinion
   Despite the protests of the entire city council, the mayor remained *adamant*.
   syn: stubborn   *ant: amenable; flexible*

7. **diffident** (dif´ i dənt) *adj.* lacking in self-confidence; shy
   The *diffident* student hated to speak in front of the class.
   syn: timid   *ant: outgoing*

8. **opus** (ō´ pəs) *n.* a creative work, especially a numbered composition
   (The plural of *opus* is *opera*)
   My favorite composition by Antonin Dvořák is *Opus* 95.

9. **ostensible** (o sten´ sə bəl) *adj.* professed but not necessarily true
The *ostensible* reason for inviting her up to his room was to show her his bottle cap collection.
syn: supposed   *ant: actual*

10. **disparity** (di spar´ i tē) *n.* inequality; difference
My wife is twelve years older than I am, but we get along well despite the *disparity* in our ages.
syn: gap   *ant: similarity*

Exercise I

Words in Context

From the list below, supply the words needed to complete the paragraph. Some words will not be used.

cliché	extol	adamant	rancor
ostensible	clement	disparity	

A.   I wish that I could _____ your recent work, but as the _____ goes, workers like you are a dime a dozen. I've been keeping you on the payroll despite your recent incompetence, but it must end now. The president is _____ about cutting unnecessary costs, so I'm afraid that I'm going to have to let you go. I wish you more _____ times in the future.

From the list below, supply the words needed to complete the paragraph. Some words will not be used.

inexorable	disparity	opus	diffident
ostensible	clement	rancor	

B.   When the manager noticed the _____ between the amount of cash in the register and the total of the nightly bank deposit, he never suspected Yvonne. _____ mild mannered and _____ in the office, she would engage in arguments filled with _____ and threats at home; her husband knew that the _____ result of her stealing would be jail. She felt, however, that one huge theft of the company payroll would be construed as the work of an outsider, not the grand, climactic _____ of her career in crime.

Exercise II

Sentence Completion

Complete the sentence in a way that shows you understand the meaning of the italicized vocabulary word.

1. Devon's *rancor* over excessive violence on TV made him...

2. The *cliché*, "to tie the knot," actually means...

3. Aunt Rita's *adamant* belief in superstition causes her to...

4. A *diffident* person will probably never become...

5. The composer's latest *opus* will be played by...

6. Carol's *ostensible* purpose was charity, but she really wanted...

7. The *disparity* among our political opinions sometimes results in...

8. The *clement* weather will...

9. The Speedy-Mart manager *extolled* Jeremy for...

10. The advance of the invading forces seemed *inexorable* until...

Exercise III

Roots, Prefixes, and Suffixes

Study the entries and answer the questions that follow.

The prefix *circum* means "around, on all sides."
The root *naviga* means "to sail, to steer."
The prefixes *intro* and *intra* mean "in, within, inside of."
The roots *spec* and *spect* mean "to see, look at."
The roots *vert* and *vers* mean "to turn."
The root *locu* means "speaking."
The prefix *extro* means "outside."

A. *Using literal translations as guidance, define the following words without using a dictionary:*

   1. circumnavigate   4. introspect
   2. retrospect   5. circumlocutions
   3. introvert   6. extrovert

B. List as many words as you can think of that contain the root *spec* and the root *vert*. Try to define each word literally.

C. List as many words as you can think of that contain the prefix *circum* and the prefix *intro*. Try to define each word literally.

Exercise IV

Inference

Complete the sentences by inferring information about the italicized word from its context.

A. Because Shelly is so *adamant* about not accepting birthday gifts, her friends could...

B. The judge was *clement* when she sentenced the offender, so the crime was probably...

C. Sierra produced twice as many widgets as needed, so her supervisor *extolled* her by...

Exercise V

Writing

Here is a writing prompt similar to the one you will find on the essay writing portion of the ACT.

How much do you value your summer break? When the American school system was established, children spent summers working on the farm, where their help was crucial. Proponents of year-round school claim that this system is antiquated, and that the traditional summer break should be divided up and spread throughout the year. Long breaks, advocates claim, cause students to forget things learned during the school year, and unused, empty school buildings are simply wasteful. Under year-round school, students would have three-week extended breaks throughout the year, as well as all the traditional holiday breaks.

Detractors of the year-round school note that year-round school will challenge extracurricular programs and summer jobs, and that the breaks would still be long enough for students to forget what they learn. Supporters point to the success of existing year-round schools in use in many states and nations.

Imagine that your school is contemplating a switch to year-round education (or reverting back to a traditional school year with a summer break, if it is already a year-round school). Take a position, and write a well-crafted letter to the school board using reasons and examples to support your opinion.

Thesis: Write a *one-sentence* response to the above assignment. Make certain this single sentence offers a clear statement of your position.

Example: If school is truly a preparation for adult life, then students should be attending it all year, as though they were working.

_____

_____

Organizational Plan: List at least three subtopics you will use to support your main idea. This list is your outline.

1. _____

2. _____

3. _____

Draft: Following your outline, write a good first draft of your essay. Remember to support all your points with examples, facts, references to reading, etc.

Review and Revise: Exchange essays with a classmate. Using the scoring guide for Sentence Formation and Variety on page 227, score your partner's essay (while he or she scores yours). Focus on sentence structure and use of language conventions. If necessary, rewrite your essay to improve the sentence structure and the use of language.

Exercise VI

English Practice

Identifying Sentence Errors
Identify the errors in the following sentences. Choose the answer that fixes the error. If the sentence contains no error, select NO CHANGE.

1. Many people go to the movies to escape reality, but <u>my best friend and me</u> go to be entertained.
    A. NO CHANGE
    B. me and my best friend
    C. I and my best friend
    D. my best friend and I

2. Everyone should have a dream <u>that they can strive</u> for, even if it sometimes seems impossible to achieve it.
    F. NO CHANGE
    G. that they strive
    H. that he or she can strive
    J. that can be striven

3. If Deanna or Katie <u>win</u> the election for class president, I'll be disappointed.
    A. NO CHANGE
    B. wins
    C. had won
    D. have a chance to win

4. Because I rely on my calculator so often, <u>I had forgotten how</u> to do long division.
   F. NO CHANGE
   G. I have forgotten how
   H. I forget how
   J. I forgot how

5. During the holidays, my family and I <u>traveled further than last year.</u>
   A. NO CHANGE
   B. traveled farther than last year.
   C. traveled farther than we did last year.
   D. traveled further than last year's holidays.

Exercise VI

English Practice

Improving Sentences
The underlined portion of each sentence below contains some flaw. Select the answer that best corrects the flaw.

6. I laughed when I saw my neighbor, Mr. Bean, <u>yelling at people in his long underwear in the street</u>
   F. yelling at people, in his long underwear, in the street
   G. yelling in the street at people, in his long underwear
   H. yelling at people in the street in his long underwear
   J. in his long underwear, yelling at people in the street

7. <u>My parents trusted me with their new car because I passed the driving test without a problem, I studied for it for more than a month.</u>
   A. My parents trusted me with their new car because I passed the driving test without a problem, but I spent more than a month studying for it.
   B. My parents trusted me with their new car because I passed the driving test without a problem, and I studied for it for more than a month.
   C. My parents trusted me with their new car because I passed the driving test without a problem, even though I had studied for it for more than a month.
   D. My parents trusted me with their new car; I studied for the driving test for more than a month. I passed it without a problem.

8. In the United States, <u>we can vote and will be able to sign contracts</u> legally at the age of 18.
    F. we can vote and then sign contracts
    G. we vote and can sign contracts
    H. we can vote and sign contracts
    J. we can vote and are permitted to sign contracts

9. <u>Do the people who use cell phones driving cause more accidents than are caused by others?</u>
    A. Do the people who use cell phones while they are driving cause more accidents than other people will do?
    B. Do the people who use cell phones driving cause more accidents than others?
    C. Do the people who use cell phones while driving cause more accidents than people who don't?
    D. Do the people who use cell phones driving cars cause more accidents than those who don't use cell phones in the car?

10. Natalie raised her voice <u>above the loud music to be heard</u>.
    F. above the loud music, so people would be able to hear her.
    G. to be heard above the loud music.
    H. above the loud music so her words could be heard.
    J. so that she would be able to be hear over the very loud music.

Vocabulary
Power Plus
for the
ACT
Vocabulary,
Reading, and Writing
Exercises for High Scores

Lesson Six

1. **condone** (kən dōn´) *v.* to forgive or overlook an offense
   After hearing about the man's starving family, most found it easy to *condone* his theft of the food.
   syn: pardon; excuse   *ant: condemn*

2. **nuance** (nōō´ äns) *n.* a slight or subtle degree of difference
   The sharpest listeners detected a *nuance* in the speaker's tone that revealed her opinion.
   syn: gradation; shade

3. **connoisseur** (kon ə sûr´) *n.* an expert in matters of culture, food, or wine
   The chef watched nervously as the *connoisseur* tasted the soup.
                                        ant: tyro; novice; neophyte

4. **enigma** (i nig´ mə) *n.* a mystery; something seemingly inexplicable
   Mona Lisa's smile is an *enigma* because no one knows the thoughts behind her inscrutable expression.
   syn: riddle; puzzle

5. **apathy** (ap´ ə thē) *n.* lack of interest; state of not caring
   The fund drive to raise money for a new gym failed because of student *apathy*.
   syn: indifference   *ant: interest; eagerness*

6. **officious** (ə fish´ əs) *adj.* excessively eager to deliver unasked for or unwanted help
   I wish my *officious* sister would stop telling me how to run my life.
   syn: meddlesome; interfering

7. **credence** (krēd´ ns) *n.* belief or trust
   Surprisingly, Shayna's teacher gave *credence* to her story about how she lost her homework.
   syn: faith; confidence   *ant: disbelief*

8. **jaunty** (jôn´ tē) *adj.* having a buoyant, self-confident air; brisk and crisp
   My three-year-old always walks in a *jaunty* manner when I put him in that sailor suit.
   syn: confident; poised

9. **dilettante** (dil i tänt´) *n.* one who merely dabbles in an art or a science
   The *dilettante* felt that his superficial knowledge of art qualified him to judge the artist's work.
   syn: amateur; trifler   *ant: expert; professional*

10. **cult** (kult) *n.* an organized group of people with an obsessive devotion to a person or set of principles
    To join the *cult*, recruits had to shave their heads and walk over burning coals.
    syn: sect

Exercise I

Words in Context

From the list below, supply the words needed to complete the paragraph. Some words will not be used.

condone	nuance	connoisseur	apathy
officious	cult	credence	dilettante

A.   The chef, tucked away in the kitchen, nervously awaited the report from the latest critic. Knowing that Mr. Tahoma was a[n] _____ of Peruvian cuisine and a weekly newspaper columnist with a[n] _____ following, the chef hoped that the waiters refrained from the _____ behavior that well-known food critics must often endure from servers. The chef had run the restaurant for twenty-eight years; he was certainly not a[n] _____ in matters of cooking, but owing to a decline in customers, he worried about the fate of the business. He could only hope that Mr. Tahoma would rave about the many subtle _____ in the meal. A positive review, combined with the _____ accorded to the column, might be all that the chef needed to save the restaurant.

From the list below, supply the words needed to complete the paragraph. Some words will not be used.

credence   condone   nuance   enigma   apathy   jaunty

B.   Though she was a hostess at the restaurant, Rolinda remained seated, even as customers entered the waiting area. Quietly expressing her _____ about hungry suburbanites, Rolinda confined herself to a sigh and let younger servers greet the new potential tippers at the door. She knew that her manager would not _____ her behavior so she took her place in front of the main table. Rolinda also wondered why, even though she hadn't been sick, she had been so tired for the last month. If she didn't solve this _____ soon, she would more than likely lose her job. For another day, she would just have to put on a fake smile and affect a[n] _____ manner until the end of her shift.

> ## Exercise II
>
> # *Sentence Completion*

Complete the sentence in a way that shows you understand the meaning of the italicized vocabulary word.

1.   Parents cannot *condone* their children's actions when…

2.   The *dilettante* never grew tired of watching the stars, hoping someday to…

3.   "This case is quite an *enigma*," said the detective. We'll be lucky to…

4.   To show their loyalty, members of the *cult* wear…

5.   The rare cadillac was at the top of the *connoisseur's* want list, so she…

6.   Giving *credence* to the refugees' story, the border guard…

7.   Never voting or reading the newspaper revealed Kenton's *apathy* for…

8.   After enduring her *officious* mother for more than thirty years, Loren decided to…

9.   Nick had a *jaunty* walk after…

10.   There was only a slight *nuance* of difference between…

Exercise III

Roots, Prefixes, and Suffixes

Study the entries and answer the questions that follow.

The root *arch* means "rule," "govern," or "to be first."
The roots *dem* and *demos* mean "people."
The roots *mit* and *mis* mean "send."
The suffix *ist* means "one who practices or believes."
The suffix *cracy* means "rule by."
The suffix *graphy* means "writing about" or "study of."

A. Using literal translations as guidance, define the following words without using a dictionary.

    1. archetype   4. demography
    2. transmit   5. monarchy
    3. democracy   6. remit

B. A technocrat would be a supporter of _____.

C. The root *oligos* means few; therefore, an oligarchy would probably be

_____.

D. List as many words as you can think of that contain the forms *arch, dem, mit, mis,* or *crat.*

E. The prefix *an* means "without" or "against." An anarchist is

_____.

Exercise IV

Inference

Complete the sentences by inferring information about the italicized word from its context.

A. The *connoisseur* refused a considerable sum to endorse the fast-food chain because she believed that...

B. When the *apathy* of your coworkers causes them to ignore your requests, the best way to get their attention is to…

C. The cause of the dog's odd behavior remains an *enigma*, so the owner will probably…

Exercise V

Critical Reading

Below is a reading passage followed by several multiple-choice questions similar to the ones you will encounter on the ACT. Carefully read the passage and choose the best answer for each of the questions.

The author of the following passage offers a view on aging that is considerably different from the view espoused by popular culture, focusing on the benefits of aging rather than the disadvantages.

We are told that by the year 2030, one of every four Americans will be at least 60 years of age, so one benefit of advancing age will be having lots of company. A secondary benefit is knowing that tasks we took on as young adults are completed, and we can enjoy our years of relaxation.

5 Our bodies have been changing throughout our lives, and growth and change have been continuous parts of maturation. As infants, we experienced a change in eye color, bone strength, tooth formation, size, and weight almost every day. Going from one stage to another is nothing new to us, but in our early growing years we were so busy waiting to be 13, 16, 18, and 21 that we were not paying much
10 attention to slight differences in our physical makeup. What changes we were aware of, such as height and physical strength, were often welcomed.

Adapting to any stage of life is common to us all, even if the changes we encounter are those found in aging. Aging is as normal as an infant's learning to walk and talk, and once accepted, no more difficult to get used to. As we all speak
15 differently, so will each of us change differently with age, and our adaptations to life as we advance will evoke as many different reactions.

Nothing really changes as far as basic needs are concerned. We will always need air, food, water, clothing, shelter, and sometimes medical care. Our handling of all these needs may change over the years as we find ourselves providing for someone
20 else, and eventually, having someone else provide for us.

Limitations in sight, hearing, and mobility may herald our continuing progression through life's stages, but as long as we are aware that there are ways of coping with every situation, we need not be apprehensive.

People are inherently independent and have a tendency toward self-sufficiency
25 that perseveres no matter the age. Our needs for companionship and feelings of self-worth never diminish because we all want to be a productive part of our world community—to see a purpose for our lives. None of us desires uselessness, and we want to feel that we will never cease to have a place in the society to which we have already made many contributions.

30   Remaining mentally alert and maintaining a high level of emotional health are paramount in adjusting to advancing age. Being socially active is an important first step in the process, and volunteerism is a good way to achieve it. Sharing experiences with those who may benefit from hearing them and offering aid to worthy causes help us to maintain a positive outlook and self-image.

35   Physical limitations or even total confinement need not hamper social involvement. Mental activities such as reading and keeping a journal are productive exercises that can be accomplished in one's own home. Interpersonal relationships can provide strong support but do not necessitate traveling away from home. The telephone has long been the device used for people to "reach out and touch
40   someone"; similarly, the computer and the Internet now offer nearly everyone the ability to keep in touch through e-mail and instant messaging technology. Restrictive physical changes should be looked at as challenges rather than hindrances and may actually bring about the learning of new practices, arts, crafts, and outward expressions of personality or hidden talents.

45   As senescence brings about changes in hearing or vision, we find these differences can be endured more readily than drastic changes in movement such as those brought on by stroke or serious accident. For hearing or vision loss, occupational therapists can make us aware of devices we can learn to rely on, or ways of enhancing remaining capabilities by placing positive importance on
50   substituting one sense for another. Taste and smell, for example, can be dependable supportive senses when vision diminishes, and touch and sight can compensate for hearing loss. Eyeglasses and hearing aids may become part of everyday attire with relative ease; however, improvements to loss of mobility may be considerably more challenging.

55   Occupational therapists can assist in regaining full or partial freedom of movement after a period of inactivity following stroke or accident. These therapists are specially trained experts who can help a person adapt to each physical challenge in ways that defy constraints of demanding situations at home or away. They can help us find new capabilities and adjust our attitudes by encouraging the natural
60   instinct for self-sufficiency and independence. Their vast knowledge of many types of equipment, such as chair elevators, mobile carts, walkers, wheelchairs, canes, and the use of heat and massage, is extremely valuable reinforcement.

    Health professionals can also lead us to make correct decisions about our care if memory loss occurs. They help us to determine whether a physical change is
65   responsible for memory problems or whether further medical attention should be sought when conditions that are more serious are suspected.

    The most important thing to keep in mind is that there are many more resources available than ever before. Aging is no longer something to be dreaded. We have access to a great deal of help from many different agencies and support groups, with
70   more sources emerging every day. Coping with changes in life has never been easy, but with so many shoulders to share the burdens, the most difficult thing we may have to do is ask for help.

1. The intention of this passage is to
    A. remind us that we will all be growing old.
    B. inform young people that they will have certain maladies later in life.
    C. reassure people that aging is not a condition to be feared.
    D. offer suggestions for what older people can do while waiting to die.

2. In the beginning of the passage, what is meant by the statement, "Going from one stage to another is nothing new to us…" (lines 7-10)?
    F. We changed from being babies to being children, to being teens, to being adults.
    G. We are accustomed to changing our addresses, our clothes, our cars, our furniture.
    H. We can live with changes in our own lives because we have seen changes in others.
    J. We are not strangers to seeing different ages, such as the ice age, the iron age, the atomic age, etc.

3. By emphasizing that adaptation is a common human trait, paragraph 3 (lines 12-16) is attempting
    A. to show that babies learn to walk, and so does everyone else.
    B. to show that there is nothing abnormal or unduly difficult in facing changes associated with aging.
    C. to show that growing old is just like learning to talk and walk for the first time.
    D. to prove that infants learn to talk in the same way as older people.

4. What is the purpose of telling us our basic needs if they remain the same (lines 17-20)?
    F. We need to be reminded that we require all the things mentioned.
    G. We need to be told we cannot survive without air, water, food, etc.
    H. A checklist can be formed using the guidelines set forth in the passage.
    J. Basic needs do not change, but our use of them does.

5. What is the best paraphrase of lines 24-25: "self-sufficiency that perseveres no matter the age?"
    A. Self-sufficiency is something we all want, no matter which era we live in.
    B. No matter how old we are, we still want to be able to take care of ourselves.
    C. No matter how we age, we are still sufficiently aware of ourselves.
    D. We persevere sufficiently at each age, no matter how old we get.

6. The word "paramount" in line 31 is used to express
   F. the highest level of our activity is mental.
   G. that mental and emotional health are the same thing.
   H. that only people with self-esteem are mentally alert.
   J. the importance of mental and emotional health.

7. The main idea of paragraph 8 (lines 35-44) is
   A. to remind us that old people can only stay at home because of physical impairment.
   B. that we shouldn't stay at home just because we get old.
   C. to show that physical impairment can lead to discovery of other capabilities.
   D. to show that we all need friends, especially at home.

8. Given the context of the passage, the word *senescence* (line 45) most nearly means
   F. a lack of interest in reading.
   G. deteriorating physical abilities.
   H. the inability to see and hear.
   J. the process of aging.

9. What is the main purpose of the last two paragraphs?
   A. They give final advice about aging, and how to seek help.
   B. They conclude the passage with a summary of information.
   C. They lead the reader to want to make notes about the passage.
   D. They offer a few final words of encouragement.

10. If the title of this passage were "Aging in America," then which choice would be the best subtitle?
    F. It's Not a Second Childhood
    G. Just Another Stage of Life
    H. Help for the Elderly
    J. Aging is Beneficial, So Get Used to It

Book Two

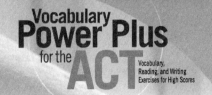

Vocabulary
Power Plus
for the **ACT**
Vocabulary,
Reading, and Writing
Exercises for High Scores

Lesson Seven

1. **cynical** (sin´ i kəl) *adj.* doubtful or distrustful of the goodness or sincerity of human motives
    Ken made the *cynical* observation that Jamie's new girlfriend was probably just interested in his money.
    syn: skeptical   *ant: idealistic; optimistic*

2. **ambivalent** (am biv´ ə lənt) *adj.* having opposing attitudes or feelings toward a person, thing, or idea; unable to decide
    Doug felt *ambivalent* about his job; although he hated the pressure, he loved the challenge.
    syn: uncertain; wavering   *ant: certain; resolute*

3. **demagogue** (dem´ ə gŏg) *n.* a leader who appeals to citizens' emotions to obtain power
    The *demagogue* evoked the sympathy of the public to justify his crimes in office.
    syn: rabble-rouser

4. **demure** (di myoor´) *adj.* quiet and modest; reserved
    Her *demure* behavior was really a ruse to cover up her criminal nature.
    syn: prim   *ant: indiscreet*

5. **intrepid** (in trep´ īd) *adj.* without fear; brave
    The *intrepid* warrior did not even flinch when the tiger leapt from the tree.
    syn: bold; fearless   *ant: cowardly*

6. **destitute** (des´ ti tōot) *adj.* extremely poor; lacking necessities like food and shelter
    Because they had no insurance, they were left *destitute* when their house burned down.
    syn: impoverished; penniless   *ant: affluent*

7. **erudite** (er´ yə dīt) *adj.* scholarly; learned
    Not much of a scholar, Justin was intimidated by his *erudite* girlfriend.
    syn: educated   *ant: unlettered; illiterate*

8. **dilemma** (di lem´ ə) *n.* a choice between two unpleasant or difficult options
    Whether to repair my old car or purchase a new one was a real *dilemma*.

9. **culmination** (kul mə nā´ shən) *n.* the highest point of attainment; the end or climax
Winning the state tournament was the *culmination* of a great basketball season.
syn: apex   *ant: nadir*

10. **concur** (kən kûr´) *v.* to be of the same opinion; to agree with
I *concur* that we should keep this meeting short.
syn: support; agree   *ant: dispute; differ*

Exercise I

Words in Context

From the list below, supply the words needed to complete the paragraph. Some words will not be used.

concur	intrepid	cynical	destitute
dilemma	ambivalent	culmination	

A. One year after the _____ of the second Mineral War, the surviving inhabitants of the Europa mining colony were _____ and malnourished. The chief engineer tried her best to restore the food reprocessing system, but, owing to the lack of replacement parts, the unit could produce only thirty percent of the colony's nutritional needs. Captain Keith remained _____ about leading a few _____ miners on a necessary but dangerous expedition to the old generation plant in the Nova Crater to salvage parts for the rapidly declining life support system. Most of the miners were _____ about their fate at the colony, and Captain Keith would have been lying if he said that he didn't _____ with their pessimistic opinions.

From the list below, supply the words needed to complete the paragraph. Some words will not be used.

culmination   demagogue   concur   erudite   dilemma   demure

B. Clayton surprised everyone in Selbyville when he entered the race for mayor. For twenty-six years, he had been the mild-mannered, _____ clerk at the Selbyville Courthouse. Well-versed in history and politics, the _____ Clayton never really struck anyone as having the type of personality required to win an election, let alone become the mayor. Word spread quickly when, during a special pre-election meeting, Clayton stood at the podium and delivered an impressive speech. Every word was loaded with passion, especially when Clayton addressed Selbyville's _____ of accepting or rejecting a controversial landfill. After ten minutes of rhetoric, Clayton had the townspeople shouting their support, and the sentiment continued right through to the election, after which Clayton became the new mayor. Three months later, the citizens of Selbyville discovered that Clayton was just a[n] _____ when construction of the new landfill began, and he mysteriously bought a new speedboat that was well beyond the range of a typical small-town mayor's salary.

Exercise II

Sentence Completion

Complete the sentence in a way that shows you understand the meaning of the italicized vocabulary word.

1. Your *cynical* attitude makes other people...

2. When forced to be in public, the *demure* Kelly...

3. Now *destitute*, the bankrupt stockbroker lives...

4. The *erudite* professor occasionally lost the attention of her students because...

5. Manny was *ambivalent* about taking the new job because...

6. Stranded behind enemy lines, the *intrepid* soldier...

7. A *demagogue* like Hitler can successfully convince people to...

8. His parents would not *concur* with Dharma's decision to...

9. The *culmination* of the symphony's season occurred at...

10. A *dilemma* at work can force a person to...

Exercise III

Roots, Prefixes, and Suffixes

Study the entries and answer the questions that follow.

The root *fid* means "faith" or "trust."
The root *form* means "shape."
The root *crea* means "create, make."
The prefix *re* means "again."
The suffix *tion* means "the act of."
The prefix *re* means "back" or "again."
The prefix *con* means "with."

A. *Using literal translations as guidance, define the following words without using a dictionary:*

   1. reformation   4. re-creation
   2. reverted   5. fidelity
   3. malformed   6. confide

B. *Infidelity* is _____.

C. The Marine Corps' motto, "Semper Fidelis," means _____
   _____.

D. List as many words as you can think of that contain the roots *fid* and *form*.

Exercise IV

Inference

Complete the sentences by inferring information about the italicized word from its context.

A. When Cynthia sees a *destitute* child, she usually...

B.   If a *demagogue* gets elected, the citizens might…

C.   During the battle, the *intrepid* soldier will probably volunteer to…

Exercise V

Writing

Here is a writing prompt similar to the one you will find on the essay writing portion of the ACT.

> Zero-tolerance policies in schools are intended to eliminate behaviors deemed intolerable, such as violence, bullying, or the carrying of weapons. Are strict policies such as these effective and necessary, or are they well-intended nonsense that cannot be enforced until after the damage is done? Consider the implications of a student being suspended for defending himself or herself against a bully, or a second-grader being expelled for having a butter knife in his or her lunchbox. Is it right to teach children to surrender themselves to the threats of bullies?
>
> Imagine a school situation in which the rule might not seem warranted, causing students to be punished unnecessarily. Explain why you either support or reject zero-tolerance policies.

Thesis: Write a *one-sentence* response to the above assignment. Make certain this single sentence offers a clear statement of your position.

Example: Extremes rarely solve problems without creating new ones, so zero-tolerance policies need to be revisited.

_____

_____

Organizational Plan: List at least three subtopics you will use to support your main idea. This list is your outline.

1. _____

2. _____

3. _____

Draft: Following your outline, write a good first draft of your essay. Remember to support all your points with examples, facts, references to reading, etc.

Review and Revise: Exchange essays with a classmate. Using the scoring guide for Word Choice on page 228, score your partner's essay (while he or she scores yours). Focus on the word choice and use of language conventions. If necessary, rewrite your essay to improve the word choice and the use of language.

Exercise VI

English Practice

Improving Paragraphs
Read the following passage and then choose the best revision for the underlined portions of the paragraph. The questions will require you to make decisions regarding the revision of the reading selection. Some revisions are not of actual mistakes, but will improve the clarity of the writing.

[1]

When you see a marathon runner stumble across the finish line, exhausted after a journey that would cause the average person to keel over dead, do you "say so what! Anyone can do that?"[1] Maybe you wouldn't. But, many[2] people would assert that yes, anyone can do it, and, as a matter of fact, we are made for it.

1. A. NO CHANGE
   B. say "So what!": anyone can do that?
   C. say "So what! anyone can do that".
   D. say, "so what! Anyone can do that"?

2. F. NO CHANGE
   G. wouldn't, but many
   H. would not; therefore,
   J. wouldn't. But many

[2]

We don't have sharp claws or long teeth to catch food or defend ourselves from predators. Sure, we have <u>the most biggest</u>[4] brains, but our average eyesight and hearing are still likely to get us into situations in which those mammals having claws, teeth, and an abundance of muscle make short work of us. <u>Their is only one thing that human beings can do better than the wild mammals: run.</u>[5] And not fast, either—certainly any bear or leopard will catch you before you even turn around; though animals will outrun humans in a sprint, however, they tire very quickly, and that's when humans gain the advantage. <u>It's the long run at which we excel,</u>[6] mainly because we are built for it.

3. Which of the following sentences would be the most appropriate introductory sentence for paragraph 2?
   A. No one can question the ability of long distance runners in comparison to most predators.
   B. In comparison to the average mammal, a person's physical ability may not seem especially impressive.
   C. In a comparison between humans and other mammals, people are not especially impressive.
   D. Modern footwear, some runners attest, is conducive to foot injury over long distances.

5. A. NO CHANGE
   B. There are many things that human beings can do better than wild mammals, and one of the best talents we have is running.
   C. One of the things that human beings can do better than wild mammals is run.
   D. There is only one thing that human beings can do better than wild mammals can: run.

6. F. NO CHANGE
   G. It is in the long run at which we excel,
   H. The long distance running is where we excel,
   J. We excel in the long run, distance running,

4. F. NO CHANGE
   G. the bigger
   H. the most
   J. the biggest

[3]

People, unlike most beasts, have the ability to sweat. Coupled with our hairless skin, sweating allows people to keep their body temperature down during long periods of effort. Our <u>cooling, ability, large knees, and elastic tendons,</u>[7] allow us to outrun a horse—in the long run, of course. That's right: over long distances, human beings can outrun almost every running mammal on earth. This ability might not have saved our ancestors from saber tooth tigers, but it provided them a distinct advantage <u>while tracking the many tasty quadrupeds living on the plains.</u>[8]

7. A. NO CHANGE
    B. cooling ability, large, knees
       and elastic tendons,
    C. ability to cool large knees
       and elastic tendons
    D. cooling ability, large knees,
       and elastic tendons

8. F. NO CHANGE
    G. while tracking the
       quadrupeds, many of which
       were tasty, living on the
       plains.
    H. while tracking the tasty
       plains animals.
    J. while they tracked down
       animals, which they knew
       were tasty, on the plains.

[4]

Antelope, like dogs, simply do not sweat; they must pant to cool its bodies. In order to pant, an animal must stop running. Animals that are being chased by hungry people with spears do not have the luxury <u>to rest and thus overheat and collapse,</u> rendering themselves easy targets for the brain-guided clubs and arrows of our jogging ancestors. To see the process for yourself, visit the Bushmen of the Kalahari Desert and follow them on a hunt, which may continue for miles over the course of days. Be sure to keep up.

9. A. NO CHANGE
    B. to rest and overheat and
       collapse
    C. of rest; then overheat and
       collapse
    D. of resting and thus overheat
       and collapse

[5]

<u>When one returns from the Kalahari, you should swing</u>[10] by the copper canyon of mexico,where the Tarahumara people play a game that involves running in a group more than fifty miles, kicking a wooden ball all the way. Leave your sneakers at home: the Tarahumara run virtually barefoot, shod in simple one-piece sandals made from thin strips of leather or rubber. The lack of overengineered footwear among the Tarahumara, especially over unpaved, natural surfaces, allows the machine of the human body to do the job <u>it is already</u>[11] perfectly adapted to do.

10. F. NO CHANGE
    G. When one returns from the Kalahari, he should swing
    H. When you return from the Kalahari, swing
    J. Returning from the Kalahari shold swing you

11. A. NO CHANGE
    B. it's now
    C. it is all ready
    D. it can be

[6]

Oddly enough, foot and leg injuries common to runners in the developed world—joint damage, shin splints, bone spurs—are practically unknown to the Tarahumara. Sneakers typically force runners to land on their heels, sending shocks throughout the <u>body. While making</u>[12] minimal use of the springlike arch and large tendons of the foot. Barefoot runners land midfoot, allowing their bodies to absorb the shock and return the energy to the stride. Granted, barefoot running on manmade surfaces might be <u>devastating to feet; people</u>,[13] after all, didn't spend 100,000 years adapting to run on blacktop and pavement.

12. F. NO CHANGE
    G. body; while making
    H. body, while making
    J. body—while making

13. A. NO CHANGE
    B. devastating to feet! people
    C. devastating to feet—People
    D. devastating to feet, people

[7]

Now, before you go out and run a marathon, know that long-distance runners don't <u>sit around for four months in between twenty-mile jaunts being sedentary and not doing anything.</u>[14] Predictably, people who run long distances can do so because they do it regularly. Most human beings might have the potential to run long distances, but that potential is not going to be actualized by couch potatoes and people who run one mile in order to loosen up for a workout. There aren't an easy way to achieve the constitution and endurance of a distance runner—<u>naturals or not, we still have to work up to it.</u>[15]

14. F. NO CHANGE
    G. sit around being sedentary for four months in between twenty-mile jaunts and not doing anything.
    H. sit around for four months in between twenty-mile jaunts not doing anything.
    J. sit around for four months in between twenty-mile jaunts.

15. A. NO CHANGE
    B. natural runners or not, humans still must work up to it.
    C. natural or not, we still have to work up to a marathon.
    D. natural runners or not, we must still work up to running a marathon.

Vocabulary
Power Plus
for the **ACT**
Vocabulary,
Reading, and Writing
Exercises for High Scores

REVIEW

Lessons 1–7

Exercise I

Sentence Completion

Choose the best pair of words to complete the sentence. Most choices will fit grammatically and will even make sense logically, but you must choose the pair that best fits the idea of the sentence.

1. Because he could not trust his own citizens, the despot ruling the tiny nation hired _____ to _____ the security forces guarding his compound.
    A. cults, castigate
    B. mercenaries, augment
    C. nuances, expunge
    D. libations, condone
    E. connoisseurs, banter

2. The _____ of fine wine was known to host _____ parties that sometimes lasted for days.
    A. argot, demure
    B. adamant, furtive
    C. anathema, jaunty
    D. connoisseur, bacchanalian
    E. demagogue, candid

3. Using her influence as a forceful speaker, the _____ turned public opinion against the business executive and _____ him into funding her political campaign.
    A. dilettante, extolled
    B. credence, extradited
    C. demagogue, coerced
    D. mercenary, abetted
    E. bastion, concurred

4. Officials removed the _____ animals from the hoarder's filthy house and charged the man with cruelty because of his _____ in caring for them.
    A. diffident, heresy
    B. emaciated, negligence
    C. copious, temerity
    D. jaunty, avarice
    E. dogmatic, culmination

5. Despite having no formal education, the leader of the _____ easily gained followers because he sounded _____ during his radio show.
    A. rancor, officious
    B. libation, ambivalent
    C. argot, dogmatic
    D. jingoism, cynical
    E. cult, erudite

6. The translation of the novel lacked sophistication and _____ resulting in a[n] _____ colorless story.
    A. nuance, insipid
    B. candid, argot
    C. ostensible, opus
    D. gregarious, bigot
    E. jaunty, culmination

7. The shuttle pilot had trained for any _____ he could expect to encounter in space except for the present one: _____ the fuel supply and be stranded in space, or keep the fuel and explode upon re-entry.
    A. temerity, extol
    B. banter, abet
    C. rancor, extradite
    D. dilemma, jettison
    E. enigma, expunge

8. The North Korean border guard noticed the tourist's _____ glance at a military vehicle, and he _____ her for attempting to spy on his nation.
    A. furtive, castigated
    B. jaunty, condoned
    C. copious, appeased
    D. meticulous, coerced
    E. cynical, extolled

Exercise II

Crossword Puzzle

Use the clues to complete the crossword puzzle. The answers consist of vocabulary words from lessons 1 through 7.

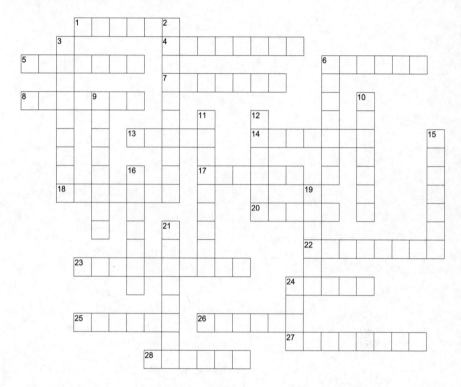

Across
1. outspoken
4. disgrace
5. secretive
6. indifference
7. scholarly
8. fort
13. disorder
14. to calm
17. hatred
18. to erase
20. to praise
22. trust
23. having opposing attitudes
24. lingo
25. easy to teach
26. modest
27. recklessness
28. confident

Down
2. amateur
3. short-tempered
6. unyielding
9. fearless
10. merciful
11. to banish
12. tactless
15. reveal
16. dull
19. agree
21. hated thing
24. to help in crime

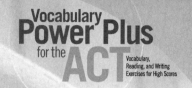
Vocabulary
Power Plus
for the
ACT
Vocabulary,
Reading, and Writing
Exercises for High Scores

Book Two

Lesson Eight

1. **abate** (ə bāt´) *v.* to lessen in violence or intensity
When the winds *abated*, the helicopter was able to land.
syn: subside; decrease   *ant: intensify; increase*

2. **decorum** (di kôr´ əm) *n.* conformity to accepted standards of conduct;
   proper behavior
The usually restless toddler surprised everyone with his *decorum* during the
ceremony.
syn: propriety   *ant: inappropriateness*

3. **abhor** (ab hôr´) *v.* to detest; to hate strongly
I *abhor* doing my laundry, so I have it professionally cleaned.
syn: despise; loathe   *ant: love; adore*

4. **dole** (dōl) *v.* to distribute; to give out sparingly
At the crowded Red Cross shelter, food was *doled* out carefully to the
earthquake victims.
                    ant: hoard

5. **gamut** (gam´ ət) *n.* the whole range or extent
Carmela's *gamut* of friends includes both overzealous socialists and greedy
capitalists.

6. **extrovert** (ek´ strə vûrt) *n.* one who is outgoing; one who is energized
   rather than drained by interactions with others
As an *extrovert*, Liz loved parties and preferred entertaining to spending a
quiet night alone.
                    ant: introvert

7. **droll** (drōl) *adj.* amusing in an odd or whimsical way
Xander had a *droll* manner of telling stories that kept everyone
entertained.
syn: quaint

8. **duplicity** (dōō plis´ i tē) *n.* intentional deceit in speech or conduct
His *duplicity* became obvious when he absent-mindedly arranged to meet
both his wife and his mistress at the same restaurant.
syn: deception   *ant: straightforwardness*

9. **effigy** (ef´ i jē) *n.* a crude dummy or image representing a hated person or group
The repressed people burned an *effigy* of their tyrannous ruler.

10. **austere** (ô stîr´) *adj.* stern; severe; plain
The judge was as *austere* in her courtroom manner as she was in her lifestyle and dress.
syn: strict; unadorned   *ant: luxurious; indulgent*

Exercise I

Words in Context

From the list below, supply the words needed to complete the paragraph. Some words will not be used.

droll   gamut   effigy   austere   duplicity   abhor   extrovert

A.   Monique was a[n] _____ who loved dealing with people, but she never thought that she would satisfy her need for socializing by selling used cars. She always _____ salespeople, but after becoming one, Monique realized that only a fraction of the salespeople indulged in the _____ and false promises that make dissatisfied customers angry enough to burn _____ of them. In fact, she enjoyed running through the _____ of sales techniques needed to close the deal.

From the list below, supply the words needed to complete the paragraph. Some words will not be used.

abate   decorum   dole   abhor   droll   austere   duplicity

B.   Typhoon Paka hammered the island of Guam for twelve hours before the winds _____. Gusts over one hundred fifty miles an hour devastated the previously green island, creating _____ living conditions for residents in the weeks to come, especially for the estimated five thousand people who lost their homes. Residents able to witness Paka in action were astounded by the serious but almost _____ sight of Paka's invisible forces tossing around automobiles, dumpsters, and palm trees as though they were children's toys. In the days following Paka, residents adhered to traditional post-typhoon _____ by cleaning up hundreds of tons of debris, checking on the condition of friends and neighbors, repairing property, and, because of the lack of electricity, hosting mass barbecues before food perished in warm refrigerators. Luckily, food was not in short supply, but water had to be _____ out by several agencies in the weeks following the tempest.

Exercise II

Sentence Completion

Complete the sentence in a way that shows you understand the meaning of the italicized vocabulary word.

1. Three days after the shipwreck, the captain *doled* out...

2. The peasants burned the *effigy* of the Duke because...

3. The comedian's *droll* attempt to impersonate the president caused...

4. The *austere* conditions on the Alaskan tundra caused the settlers to...

5. Othello trusted his wife until Iago's *duplicity* made the Moor think that...

6. The epidemic finally *abated*, and the doctors...

7. Kenyon, an *extrovert*, called all her friends and...

8. Having no time for *decorum*, the federal agents charged into the ballroom and...

9. I did *abhor* violence, so I never...

10. The *gamut* of people on the elevator ran from...

Exercise III

Roots, Prefixes, and Suffixes

Study the entries and answer the questions that follow.

The roots *frag* and *fract* mean "break."
The root *chrono* means "time."
The suffix *ment* means "the result of" or "product of the action."
The suffix *logical* means "ordered by."
The prefix *re* means "back, again."

A. *Using literal translations as guidance, define the following words without using a dictionary:*

1. chronic
2. fragment
3. fragile
4. chronological
5. chronicle
6. refract

B. A character answering a telephone during the play *Julius Caesar* would be an *anachronism* because _____.

C. A *fragmentary* report is one that is _____.

D. List as many words as you can think of that contain the forms *frag, fract,* and *chrono.*

Exercise IV

Inference

Complete the sentences by inferring information about the italicized word from its context.

A. To fashion a detailed *effigy* of the mayor, the angry townspeople might...

B. As the wagon train moved west, conditions on the plains became so *austere* that the pioneers...

C. If you *abhor* getting muddy and dirty, then you should probably not...

Exercise V

Critical Reading

Below is a reading passage followed by several multiple-choice questions similar to the ones you will encounter on the ACT. Carefully read the passage and choose the best answer to each of the questions.

This passage provides the reasons America declared itself independent from Great Britain.

When in the Course of human events it becomes necessary for one people to dissolve the political bands which have connected them with another and to assume among the powers of the earth, the separate and equal station to which the Laws of Nature and of Nature's God entitle them, a decent respect to the opinions of mankind
5　requires that they should declare the causes which impel them to the separation.

We hold these truths to be self-evident, that all men are created equal, that they are endowed by their Creator with certain unalienable Rights, that among these are Life, Liberty and the pursuit of Happiness. — That to secure these rights, Governments are instituted among Men, deriving their just powers from
10　the consent of the governed, — That whenever any Form of Government becomes destructive of these ends, it is the Right of the People to alter or to abolish it, and to institute new Government, laying its foundation on such principles and organizing its powers in such form, as to them shall seem most likely to effect their Safety and Happiness. Prudence, indeed, will dictate that Governments long established should
15　not be changed for light and transient causes; and accordingly all experience hath shewn that mankind are more disposed to suffer, while evils are sufferable than to right themselves by abolishing the forms to which they are accustomed. But when a long train of abuses and usurpations, pursuing invariably the same Object evinces a design to reduce them under absolute Despotism, it is their right, it is their duty,
20　to throw off such Government, and to provide new Guards for their future security. — Such has been the patient sufferance of these Colonies; and such is now the necessity which constrains them to alter their former Systems of Government. The history of the present King of Great Britain is a history of repeated injuries and usurpations, all having in direct object the establishment of an absolute Tyranny
25　over these States. To prove this, let Facts be submitted to a candid world.

He has refused his Assent to Laws, the most wholesome and necessary for the public good.

He has forbidden his Governors to pass Laws of immediate and pressing importance, unless suspended in their operation till his Assent should be obtained;
30　and when so suspended, he has utterly neglected to attend to them.

He has refused to pass other Laws for the accommodation of large districts of people, unless those people would relinquish the right of Representation in the Legislature, a right inestimable to them and formidable to tyrants only.

He has called together legislative bodies at places unusual, uncomfortable, and
35　distant from the depository of their Public Records, for the sole purpose of fatiguing them into compliance with his measures.

[...]

He has erected a multitude of New Offices, and sent hither swarms of officers to harass our people and eat out their substance.

40   He has dissolved Representative Houses repeatedly, for opposing with manly firmness his invasions on the rights of the people.

[...]

He has plundered our seas, ravaged our coasts, burnt our towns, and destroyed the lives of our people.

45   He is at this time transporting large Armies of foreign Mercenaries to compleat the works of death, desolation, and tyranny, already begun with circumstances of Cruelty & Perfidy scarcely paralleled in the most barbarous ages, and totally unworthy the Head of a civilized nation.

He has constrained our fellow Citizens taken Captive on the high Seas to
50   bear Arms against their Country, to become the executioners of their friends and Brethren, or to fall themselves by their Hands.

He has excited domestic insurrections amongst us, and has endeavoured to bring on the inhabitants of our frontiers, the merciless Indian Savages whose known rule of warfare, is an undistinguished destruction of all ages, sexes and conditions.

55   In every stage of these Oppressions We have Petitioned for Redress in the most humble terms: Our repeated Petitions have been answered only by repeated injury. A Prince, whose character is thus marked by every act which may define a Tyrant, is unfit to be the ruler of a free people.

Nor have We been wanting in attentions to our British brethren. We have
60   warned them from time to time of attempts by their legislature to extend an unwarrantable jurisdiction over us. We have reminded them of the circumstances of our emigration and settlement here. We have appealed to their native justice and magnanimity, and we have conjured them by the ties of our common kindred to disavow these usurpations, which would inevitably interrupt our connections
65   and correspondence. They too have been deaf to the voice of justice and of consanguinity. We must, therefore, acquiesce in the necessity, which denounces our Separation, and hold them, as we hold the rest of mankind, Enemies in War, in Peace Friends.

We, therefore, the Representatives of the united States of America, in General
70   Congress, Assembled, appealing to the Supreme Judge of the world for the rectitude of our intentions, do, in the Name, and by Authority of the good People of these Colonies, solemnly publish and declare, That these united Colonies are, and of Right ought to be Free and Independent States, that they are Absolved from all Allegiance to the British Crown, and that all political connection between them
75   and the State of Great Britain, is and ought to be totally dissolved; and that as Free and Independent States, they have full Power to levy War, conclude Peace, contract Alliances, establish Commerce, and to do all other Acts and Things which Independent States may of right do. — And for the support of this Declaration, with a firm reliance on the protection of Divine Providence, we mutually pledge to each
80   other our Lives, our Fortunes, and our sacred Honor.

1. In the context of the passage, what is the closest synonym of *evinces* as it appears in line 18?
   A. thwarts
   B. shows
   C. allows
   D. rejects

2. The "he" of line 26 is
   F. The leader of the colonial militia
   G. The king of Great Britain
   H. The president of Continental Congress
   J. The chancellor to the king

3. The overall tone of the passage can best be described as
   A. indifferent.
   B. hysterical.
   C. stern.
   D. emotional.

4. What is the effect of the parallel structure used in all paragraphs from lines 26-49?
   F. It focuses the blame squarely on the British king.
   G. It outlines the various misdeeds of the British government.
   H. It emphasizes the suffering of the American colonies.
   J. It lends a grave, rational tone to the entire passage.

5. The authors of this document describe the king of Britain as
   A. decent in all respects, except for taxation.
   B. having an unreasonable claim to America.
   C. the product of a biased parliament.
   D. an unjust, totalitarian dictator.

6. Based on the context of the passage, the best definition of *usurpations* (line 18) is
   F. injustices.
   G. seizures.
   H. lies.
   J. treacheries.

7. Who is the intended audience of the passage?
    A. the American colonists
    B. the king of England
    C. the French ambassador
    D. the world at large

8. Which word below is used to make the British troops seem less human?
    F. "tyrants" (line 33)
    G. "swarms" (line 38)
    H. "burnt" (line 43)
    J. "ravaged" (line 43)

9. Select the choice that best paraphrases the following sentence (lines 31-33):

    He has refused to pass other Laws for the accommodation of large districts of people, unless those people would relinquish the right of Representation in the Legislature, a right inestimable to them and formidable to tyrants only.

    A. The king would not pass any law dealing with the colonists if they demanded representation, which they claimed as a right.
    B. The king refused to plan residential areas in cities unless the people voted for his personally chosen candidates, a right no one understands, except for the king.
    C. The president of the Continental Congress refused to pass laws without the consent of urban populations, because only tyrants would allow law to be written without representation of the people.
    D. If he relinquishes the throne, the colonists will obey the laws.

10. Lines 14 through 17 suggest that the general attitude toward separation is one of
    F. eagerness.
    G. spite.
    H. reluctance.
    J. relief.

Vocabulary
Power Plus
for the
ACT
Vocabulary,
Reading, and Writing
Exercises for High Scores

Book Two

Lesson Nine

1. **emulate** (em´ yə lāt) *v.* to strive to be equal to; to imitate
   Jonas *emulated* his older brother by pursuing a career in the military.
   syn: copy

2. **sere** (sēr) *adj.* dry and withered
   After two weeks without water, the *sere* plant broke at the stem.
   syn: desiccated; arid   *ant: lush*

3. **enhance** (en hans´) *v.* to increase the value or beauty of something
   The soft, shimmering moonlight *enhanced* the beauty of the sparkling
   lake.
   syn: improve; heighten   *ant: diminish; decrease*

4. **contrite** (kən trīt´) *adj.* feeling regret for having committed some
     wrongdoing
   The *contrite* child wished she had never thought of playing baseball near
   the greenhouse.
   syn: repentant; remorseful   *ant: shameless; unrepentant*

5. **magnanimous** (mag nan´ ə məs) *adj.* noble; generous in forgiving; free
     from petty feelings or acts
   Allowing the man who had insulted him to stay for dinner was a
   magnanimous gesture on Robert's part.
   syn: generous   *ant: petty; mean*

6. **enunciate** (i nun´ sē āt) *v.* to state clearly and distinctly; to pronounce
   The speech teacher constantly reminded her students to *enunciate* their
   words carefully.
   syn: articulate

7. **collaborate** (kə lab´ ə rāt) *v.* to work with another toward a goal
   The lyricist and composer *collaborated* on the stage musical.
   syn: cooperate

8. **impound** (im pownd´) *v.* to confine; to retain in legal custody
   The police *impounded* Dave's car after they found traces of cocaine on the
   upholstery.
   syn: confiscate   *ant: release*

9. **impeccable** (im pek´ ə bəl) *adj.* faultless; without sin or blemish
Karl's appearance was *impeccable*, from his polished shoes to his neatly combed hair.
syn: immaculate; faultless; irreproachable   *ant: fallible; blameworthy*

10. **evoke** (i vōk´) *v.* to summon forth
The comedian was unable to *evoke* much of a response from the crowd.
syn: conjure up; elicit

11. **inane** (in ān´) *adj.* without sense or meaning; silly
Still dazed from the head injury, Catherine made only *inane* comments.
syn: foolish; insipid   *ant: significant; meaningful*

12. **unctuous** (ungk´ chōō əs) *adj.* exaggeratedly or insincerely polite
The salesman kept calling me "ma'am" in such an *unctuous* tone that I did not trust him for a minute.
syn: oily   *ant: genuine; sincere*

13. **expatriate** (eks pā´ trē ət) *n.* someone who chooses to live outside of, or renounce, his or her native country
Although T. S. Eliot was born in America, he was an *expatriate* for most of his life and is often considered British.

14. **frowzy** (frow´ zē) *adj.* unkempt
The lady's *frowzy* hair was so tangled that it looked like Spanish moss.
syn: slovenly   *ant: tidy*

15. **heinous** (hā´ nəs) *adj.* hatefully or shockingly evil
The jury was shocked by the young woman's *heinous* crimes.
syn: abhorrent; horrid

Lesson Nine

Nine*

Exercise I

Words in Context

From the list below, supply the words needed to complete the paragraph. Some words will not be used.

| magnanimous | impeccable | impound | contrite |
| expatriate | emulate | collaborate | |

A. "Don't _____ me, kid—unless you want to spend time in the slammer, too," Buddy laughed as he put his hands in the air and glanced around. "But if you're really interested, maybe we can _____ on 'helping' you pick the winning horse."

Lucas didn't return his uncle's smirk, and buddy became _____. Lucas never really adapted to conversing through a sheet of Plexiglas, and the tinny sound of Buddy's musing through the two-way intercom made him uncomfortable. Lucas came to the prison only because the police were going to _____ Buddy's car if no one removed it from the credit union parking lot, and Lucas thought that he was being _____ by mentioning that he, like Buddy, had an interest in horse racing.

From the list below, supply the words needed to complete the paragraph. Some words will not be used.

| evoke | expatriate | heinous | frowzy |
| inane | sere | enhance | enunciate |

B. Jerry squinted and ran his hand through his _____ mop of hair. The Pacific sun was already high in the sky, and he had a lot of work to accomplish before his guests arrived that evening. Originally from a Minnesota dairy, Jerry had lived on the tiny Micronesian island for over sixteen years. He never really considered himself to be a[n] _____, but then again, he didn't plan to return to the United States, either. Thinking that it might be a good idea to _____ his front yard before his visitors arrived, Jerry grabbed a machete and walked to the coconut grove in front of his shack. Huffing, Jerry chopped at the _____, withered fronds hanging against the trunks of the palm trees. When he finished cutting the fronds, he gathered the stray coconuts—some months old—and piled them in the corner of his yard. The yard looked sharp, even with Jerry's dilapidated shack in the background. As a bonus, Jerry decided to place two rows of tiki-torches along the path to the shack. Jerry thought that such trinkets were _____, but he wanted his two nieces from Cleveland to get the total island experience.

From the list below, supply the words needed to complete the paragraph. Some words will not be used.

enunciate   evoke   expatriate   unctuous   heinous   impeccable

C.   Jordan sat at the helm and surveyed the broken radio before speaking to Candace.

"This is not going to be easy. You're going to have to _____ all the strength you have in order to succeed."

In her typical sarcastic manner, Candace responded to Jordan in a[n] _____ tone. "Oh, really? Thank goodness you told me; I thought that swimming two miles through an oil slick would be easy!"

Candace walked over to the porthole and looked at the horizon. The line where the earth met the sky was tilted by at least seven or eight degrees; the *Nittany* was definitely taking on water. The wounded tanker in the distance wasn't doing much better; from the *Nittany's* bridge, Jordan could tell where the tanker's hull had ruptured by a black swirl slowly meandering through the crystal clear water.

"Do you remember what you're doing?"

Still annoyed, Candace _____ the directions as though she were reciting letters in an elementary school spelling bee: "Swim to the reef, walk to the shore, find the radio house, neutralize the guard, and call Boswell. Right?"

"Right," said Jordan. "Be sure to give him the proper coordinates; I'm not going down with the ship."

"Oh, don't worry," snapped Candace. "Any shark that eats you will immediately spit you back out."

"Ha-ha. Thanks for the _____ image of my certain death."

"Oh, relax. Once we get out of this, I'll treat you to a[n] _____ prepared lobster dinner on Maui. See ya later!" With that, Candace walked out of the bridge and jumped over the handrail. Jordan didn't even hear the splash.

Exercise II

Sentence Completion

Complete the sentence in a way that shows you understand the meaning of the italicized vocabulary word.

1. The *sere* peach tree finally collapsed because…

2. Some people try to *enhance* their looks by…

3. Police *impounded* Shauna's car because she…

4. The bandit's *heinous* record included the crimes of…

5. Known to be a shrine of *impeccable* art, Marlene's home was filled with…

6. The *expatriate* writer decided never to return to…

7. In his typical *magnanimous* manner, Richard ignored his sister's habitual…

8. Your *inane* behavior is not acceptable during…

9. The *frowzy* old man had obviously been living…

10. Please *enunciate* your words clearly so that everyone will…

11. Expect an *unctuous* greeting from the maitre d' if you…

12. The old medium attempted to *evoke* the spirit of…

13. The Army and the Air Force must *collaborate* during…

14. The *contrite* thief apologized for…

15. Maggie *emulates* her older sister by…

Exercise III

Roots, Prefixes, and Suffixes

Study the entries and answer the questions that follow.

> The root *cogn* means "know" or "think."
> The root *carn* means "flesh."
> The root *vor* means "eat."
> The prefix *in* means "not." (It can also mean "in.")
> The prefix *re* means "again."

A. *Using literal translations as guidance, define the following words without using a dictionary:*

1. incognito   4. carnivore
2. cogitation   5. carnivorous
3. cognizant   6. reincarnate

B. In the Latin phrase "cogito ergo sum," *ergo* means "therefore" and *sum* means "I am." What do you suppose the entire phrase means?

C. A carnival used to refer specifically to a holiday or holidays that took place just before the start of Lent. Since Lent was a time when eating meat was forbidden, what do you suppose *carnival* meant?

D. List as many words as you can think of that contain the forms *cogn, carn.*

Exercise IV

Inference

Complete the sentences by inferring information about the italicized word from its context.

A. Kayla wants to *enhance* the appearance of her room, so she should…

B. Despite her lifelong stutter, Tara *enunciated* her speeches so well that she became…

C. Dalton's older brother is a fireman, and Dalton used to *emulate* him by…

Exercise V

Writing

Here is a writing prompt similar to the one you will find on the essay writing portion of the ACT.

It is no secret that the United States, among all nations of the free world, is one of the least enthusiastic about teaching, or learning, foreign languages, even amid new heights in global economies and the rise of international communication through the internet, films, and literature.

How important is it, if at all, to learn a foreign language? Many schools require two to four years of foreign language study, but often that is not enough to foster fluency. Should schools mandate foreign language fluency? Write a letter to the Secretary of Education that outlines your argument. Support your stance with at least three reasons explaining why you think foreign language fluency should or should not be a priority in primary and secondary education. Your motive in writing the letter, for the purpose of this exercise, is to either appropriate or spare millions of dollars in Federal funds—tax dollars—for a nationwide program.

Thesis: Write a *one-sentence* response to the above assignment. Make certain this single sentence offers a clear statement of your position.

> *Example: While the merits of learning more than one language are unquestionable, they are not worth purchasing for the price of national debt.*

_____

_____

Organizational Plan: List at least three subtopics you will use to support your main idea. This list is your outline.

1. _____

2. _____

3. _____

Draft: Following your outline, write a good first draft of your essay. Remember to support all your points with examples, facts, references to reading, etc.

Review and Revise: Exchange essays with a classmate. Using the Holistic scoring guide on page 229, score your partner's essay (while he or she scores yours). If necessary, rewrite your essay to correct the problems noted by your partner.

Exercise VI

English Practice

Identifying Sentence Errors
Identify the errors in the following sentences. Choose the answer that fixes the error. If the sentence contains no error, select NO CHANGE.

1. High levels of air pollution <u>causes</u> damage to the respiratory tract.
    A. NO CHANGE
    B. can cause
    C. cause
    D. cause's

2. <u>Yesterday, we walked nearly three miles, swam a mile, or two, ran for almost an hour, and lifted some weights,</u> but we lost only a pound apiece.
    F. NO CHANGE
    G. Yesterday, we walked nearly three miles, swam a mile or two, ran for almost an hour, and lifted some weights,
    H. Yesterday, we walked nearly three miles, swam a mile, or two, ran for almost an hour, and lifted some weights,
    J. Yesterday we walked nearly three miles, swam a mile, or two, ran for almost an hour, and lifted some weights,

3. Each flower, tree, shrub, and bush <u>need watering</u>.
    A. NO CHANGE
    B. need watered
    C. need a watering
    D. needs watering

4. <u>I wrote to him, therefore he wrote back.</u>
    F. NO CHANGE
    G. I wrote to him; therefore he wrote back.
    H. I wrote to him; therefore, he wrote back.
    J. I wrote to him, and he wrote back.

5. Last year, <u>my friend Michelle and myself</u> worked in the shoe factory.
    A. NO CHANGE
    B. my friend, Michelle, and I,
    C. my friend Michelle and I
    D. me and my friend Michelle

Improving Sentences

The underlined portion of each sentence below contains some flaw. Select the answer choice that best corrects the flaw.

6. John <u>was, not only a talented student, but he also was a great athlete.</u>
   F. was not only a talented student, but also a great athlete.
   G. was only a talented student but also, he was a great athlete.
   H. was not only a talented student but in addition, he was great at athletics.
   J. was not only a talented student but was a great athlete.

7. My niece could not be <u>persuaded that giving is as much a joy as to receive</u>.
   A. persuaded that giving is as much a joy as receiving.
   B. persuaded that to give is as much a joy as receiving.
   C. believed that giving is as much of a joy as to receive.
   D. made to feel that giving is as much a joy as to receive.

8. Our leaders <u>believe and live by the law.</u>
   F. believe in and live by the law.
   G. believe in and live the law.
   H. obey and live by the law.
   J. trust and obey by the law.

9. <u>The Earth is bluer than any planets in our solar system.</u>
   A. The Earth is bluer than any planet's in our solar system.
   B. The Earth is bluer than a planets in our system.
   C. The Earth is bluer than any other planet in our solar system.
   D. The Earth is bluer than any planet in our solar system.

10. In addition, we felt that <u>she sitting</u> in as chairperson would be satisfactory.
   F. Not all pottery is antique.
   G. she's sitting in
   H. her sitting in
   J. taking the position

Vocabulary
Power Plus
for the **ACT**
Vocabulary,
Reading, and Writing
Exercises for High Scores

Lesson Ten

1. **expound** (ik spownd´) *v.* to explain in detail; to clarify
   Closing the Bible, the minister *expounded* on the passage he had just read.
   syn: elaborate   *ant: muddle; confuse*

2. **cajole** (kə jōl´) *v.* to persuade with false promises and flattery
   Despite her best efforts, the mayor could not *cajole* Madame Harris into
   donating the land to the city.
   syn: coax; wheedle   *ant: dissuade; deter*

3. **inscrutable** (in skrōō´ tə bəl) *adj.* not easily understood; hard to
   fathom
   The crazed stalker left an *inscrutable* message on my answering machine.
   syn: enigmatic   *ant: obvious; evident*

4. **balk** (bôk) *v.* to refuse stubbornly or abruptly; to stop short and
   refuse to go on
   Although Paul desperately needed the money, he *balked* at the idea of
   working for less than minimum wage.
   syn: hesitate; object   *ant: agree; continue*

5. **acrimony** (a´ krə mō nē) *n.* ill-natured, bitter hostility
   Because of his *acrimony*, the old man found himself lonely and friendless.
   syn: animosity   *ant: friendliness*

6. **dour** (dowr) *adj.* stern and ill-humored
   The librarian's *dour* expression and stereotypical bifocals contradicted her
   tattoos and noisy motorcycle.
   syn: forbidding   *ant: pleasant*

7. **exult** (ig zult´) *v.* to rejoice; to feel triumphant
   When the results were announced, the town wildly *exulted* in its team's
   victory.
   syn: celebrate

8. **omniscient** (om nish´ ənt) *adj.* having unlimited knowledge; all-knowing
   Dad described Santa Claus as an *omniscient* old man who knew whether we
   had been bad or good this year.

9. **feasible** (fē´ zə bəl) *adj.* reasonable; capable of being carried out
Though he is still young, Jeff has a *feasible* plan to participate in the Olympic games.
syn: possible; doable   *ant: unworkable*

10. **fiasco** (fē as´ kō) *n.* a complete, ridiculous failure
Our first date was a *fiasco*: I lost a contact lens, we got mugged, and a child threw up on Amber's shoes in the subway.
syn: disaster   *ant: success*

11. **métier** (me tyā´) *n.* the work one is especially suited for; one's specialty; an occupation
Justin is a decent singer, but dancing is his real *métier*.
syn: forte   *ant: weakness*

12. **fluctuate** (fluk´ chōō āt) *v.* to rise and fall; to vary irregularly
The stock market *fluctuates* so much that it seems silly to get upset when your stock goes down; it will probably go back up tomorrow.
syn: waver; vacillate   *ant: stabilize*

13. **harry** (har´ ē) *v.* to annoy or harass
The baby's constant crying began to *harry* the other passengers on the train.
syn: bother; pester   *ant: soothe*

14. **incognito** (in kog nē´ tō) *adj.* disguised; pretending not to be oneself
To avoid clamoring fans, the actor donned a disguise and traveled *incognito*.

15. **lethargy** (leth´ ər jē) *n.* lack of energy; sluggishness
The heat and humidity made me sink into the couch, too overwhelmed with *lethargy* to move.
syn: torpor; lassitude   *ant: vigor; vitality*

Exercise I

Words in Context

From the list below, supply the words needed to complete the paragraph. Some words will not be used.

fluctuate   cajole   expound   acrimony

exult   inscrutable   métier   harry

A.   Councilwoman Moore stepped up to the podium. "I don't think I need to _____ upon reasons for voting against the proposed construction; I thought that the message was clear enough at the last meeting—when you all opposed it as well. Obviously, someone has _____ a few of you into changing your opinion since last month, and your sudden, _____ decision to yield to Beta-Rad Enterprises bothers me a great deal. What happened to the surplus of _____ toward Beta-Rad from the last meeting? Don't you remember how we _____ in our victory over the radioactive waste dump? For two years, we've listened to Beta-Rad executives _____ us, and we finally had the chance to stop it for good. How could the opinions of fifteen people possibly _____ this much?"

From the list below, supply the words needed to complete the paragraph. Some words will not be used.

incognito   feasible   dour   fiasco   métier

lethargy   balk   omniscient   harry

B.   "Hey, Jye; I think you've found your _____."
      "Could be." Jye glanced up only long enough to catch a glimpse of Neve. Typing rapidly, Jye intermittently glanced at the stack of printed matrixes next to the keyboard. Usually a[n] _____ person who remained hidden in his software-engineer cubicle all day, Jye adopted a manner bordering on cynicism and _____—getting him to do tech support beyond his cubicle walls was often a[n] _____ that created more trouble than it solved. Neve was caught completely off-guard when Jye didn't _____ at the company's request that he test the system's network security by hacking into the company database. Though Jye had his ways, everyone knew that he was the _____ office authority when it came to network security protocol. It simply wouldn't have been _____ to use anyone else to test the integrity of Pentacode's newest software. Additionally, Jye's newfound energy changed his manner so much that he might as well have been _____ to those who didn't see him every day; when his attitude changed, his wardrobe and hairstyle changed as well.

Exercise II

Sentence Completion

Complete the sentence in a way that shows you understand the meaning of the italicized vocabulary word.

1. Finally able to dismount from his bicycle, Lance did not *exult* despite...

2. The monkeys, native to India, sometimes *harry* villagers by...

3. Ann's *lethargy* was not due to the heat; she was simply...

4. Caitlyn, a remarkable writer, found her *métier* as...

5. The wedding went well, but the *acrimony* between the families resulted in...

6. Please *expound* on your explanation of...

7. The *inscrutable* actions of the building inspector caused...

8. To avoid a *fiasco* during your camping trip, be sure to...

9. I would have donated money, but I *balked* when I learned that...

10. If the warden were indeed *omniscient*, then he would know that...

11. Uncle Tony was not originally a *dour* man; ten years ago, he...

12. Milton's *fluctuating* condition prevents the doctor from...

13. Not even six years of *cajoling* could convince Mrs. Garcia to...

14. Wary of being discovered by the rebels, the *incognito* Colonel Lito...

15. A *feasible* reason for missing work would be...

Exercise III

Roots, Prefixes, and Suffixes

Study the entries and answer the questions that follow.

> The root *agri* means "field, farming."
> The suffixes *ous* and *ose* mean "full of."
> The root *bell* means "war."
> The root *gere* means "bearing" or "waging."
> The prefix *ante* means "before."
> The suffix *onomy* means "study of."

A. *Using literal translations as guidance, define the following words without using a dictionary:*

    1. antebellum   4. belligerent
    2. bellicose   5. anteroom
    3. agriculture   6. agronomy

B. The roots *ces* and *ced* mean "to go"; therefore, an *antecedent* is a word that
_____ .

C. An industrial society is characterized by cities and manufacturing; an *agrarian* society is characterized by _____ .

D. List as many words as you can think of that contain the forms *agr* or *ante*.

Exercise IV

Inference

Complete the sentences by inferring information about the italicized word from its context.

A. If you *harry* the stray dog, it's quite possible that it will...

B. If an *avid* skier crashes on the slope, you can assume that...

C. Mom must have been *omniscient* if she knew that Derek secretly...

Exercise V

Critical Reading

Below is a reading passage followed by several multiple-choice questions similar to the ones you will encounter on the ACT. Carefully read the passage and choose the best answer to each of the questions.

The author of this passage is discussing the Victorian Era in Great Britain.

Despite its cruel working conditions and mass poverty, Victorian England will always be remembered as a forerunner to the modern industrial society. As an incubator for early industry, 19th century England was the first dominion in the world to experience the cultural byproducts that accompanied advancements in
5   transportation and technology. The resulting cultural shifts spawned a bouquet of unique historical attributes that today classify Victorian England.

Railways—the new method of mass land transportation to meet the blooming demands of early mass production—were at the heart of Victorian England's changes. Stimulating industry, railroads inspired advancements in coal mining, iron
10   production, and construction engineering that resulted in better buildings, bridges, and machines; these advancements, in turn, made England the foremost machine-manufacturer in the world.

As the demand for industry increased, so did the demand for a working class: skilled artisans, craftsmen, and domestic out-workers who didn't require the
15   construction of more facilities. The boom in skilled workers created a demand for more middle class members such as doctors, bankers, and lawyers. Manufacturing also caused growth in the middle class due to requirements for educated professionals such as architects, engineers, and owners of industry.

The growth and importance of the new working class caused many of the British
20   to question the justification of the existing class structure, in which the upper class appeared to reap the most benefits without having to endure the subhuman conditions of early factories. Realizing that they were crucial to industry, workers demonstrated their importance by organizing strikes in an effort to obtain better wages and working conditions. Forerunners of this movement were the Chartists,
25   who not only wanted to enhance working conditions but also to redesign the government of England. The Chartists failed to change Parliament, but they did succeed in persuading Parliament to pass several acts from 1833 to 1847 that improved working conditions for women and children.

The literature of England reflected the new social consciousness of the Victorian
30   period. Mass manufacturing led to cheap publishing, making books available for the increasingly literate masses, regardless of economic class. Owing to the availability of books, novels became popular and the prevalent subjects of literature changed. In a departure from Romantic literature, fiction entertained contemporary affairs and common people instead of ancient legends and kingly heroes. Writers such as Lewis
35   Carroll and Charles Dickens were free to satirize the establishment or to depict the austere lives that many of the working class endured every day.

New schools of thought also emerged because of the new, convenient way to

distribute information, often to the benefit of the working class. Activists such as the
Chartists explored new or better forms of government, drawing ideas from people and
40 events throughout the world, one of whom was Karl Marx. In 1840, Karl Marx wrote the
Communist Manifesto while workers were at the depths of misery. Marx's ideas favored the
strength of the workers rather than the ingenuity of industry leaders, which immediately
became an inspiration to many deprived workers. The American Revolution also fueled
sentiment in Victorian England, especially now that the middle class could read about
45 the exploits of American Revolutionary leaders and their ideas about human equality and
inherent rights. Penny magazines, cheap to produce and easy to distribute, helped inflame
the passions of the working class. New philosophies emerged as well, some of which
exemplified the legitimacy of science. Charles Darwin's *The Origin of Species*, published
in 1859, caused sudden doubt in traditional modes of thought; some people embraced
50 Positivism, which states that concrete evidence and scientific laws govern the universe.

The changing perspectives of Victorian England also inspired artists and
architects to depart from traditional styles. Designers abandoned classical décor for
Gothic spires or gaudy embellishments and stained glass windows, creating unique
designs that, to this day, many people easily identify as Victorian. Like the dividing
55 social classes, artists also held to different opinions about the role of art. Some
artists, threatened by the growth of industry, thought that art should remind people
that they are human beings and not machines. Other Victorian artists debated over
whether to maintain a classical style or to embrace realism. Like literature, new
forms of art were in high demand owing to the growing middle-class audience.
60 The railways of Victorian England carried much more than simple cargo and
passengers; they carried the sweeping changes that would blanket the world in a
new era—the Industrial Age—and it would last more than 200 years, until factories
and railways would slowly disintegrate as technology carried humans into the
Age of Information. The remnants from the era will continue to stand, however,
65 in the form of Gothic cathedrals, Queen Anne homes, and miles of steel bridges
constructed in a time when human effort was meant to be timeless.

1. The primary purpose of this passage is to
    A. explain Victorianism.
    B. discuss the impact of industry on culture.
    C. offer a theory on the "Age of the Railway."
    D. discuss the characteristics of Victorianism.

2. The overall tone of this passage is
    F. informative.
    G. descriptive.
    H. thoughtful.
    J. speculative.

3. As used in line 14, the phrase *domestic out-workers* most likely means
    A. outdoor workers.
    B. people who work from their homes.
    C. people who are no longer domestic.
    D. foreigners who work in England.

4. As used in line 33, the term *Romantic* most likely refers to
    F. the condition of being in love.
    G. the time period immediately preceding the Victorian Era.
    H. the art and philosophy of ancient Rome.
    J. involvement with poetry.

5. According to lines 29-36, which of the following helped the novel to become popular?
    A. inexpensive publishing
    B. a more literate population
    C. coal mining
    D. ink production techniques

6. According to this passage, which is *not* one of the advancements due to railroads?
    F. iron production
    G. automobile manufacturing
    H. construction engineering
    J. better bridges

7. As used in line 50, "Positivism" most likely means
    A. being attracted to the optimistic.
    B. believing provable data is the basis for knowledge.
    C. believing that everything is possible.
    D. believing only the strong survive.

8. Which of the following is *not* discussed in the passage as contributing to the characteristics of the Victorian age?
    F. an increase in industry and machines
    G. art
    H. architecture
    J. clothing styles

9. Which statement best describes the relationship between the Victorian Era and the Industrial Age?
    A. The elements of Victorian England helped lead the world into the Industrial Age.
    B. Without the fallout from the Industrial Age, Victorian England would have been bereft of art and science.
    C. Improvements in transportation allowed new art and philosphy to migrate to England during the Victorian Age.
    D. Victorian England is really a product of the social, scientific, and philosphical changes brought about by the Industrial Age.

10. This passage would most likely be found in
    F. a teen magazine.
    G. an encyclopedia of politics.
    H. a British history book.
    J. a book on architecture.

Vocabulary
Power Plus
for the
ACT
Vocabulary,
Reading, and Writing
Exercises for High Scores

Lesson Eleven

1. **epistle** (i pis´ əl) *n.* a letter or literary composition in letter form
Brian spent years writing lengthy, unsent *epistles* to his old girlfriend.

2. **avid** (av´ id) *adj.* enthusiastic; extremely interested
Dori was such an *avid* reader that I had a hard time recommending a title she had not yet read.
syn: voracious; eager   *ant: apathetic*

3. **gadfly** (gad´ flī) *n.* an irritating and persistent person
I tried to lose Judy, an obnoxious *gadfly*, in the crowd, but she stuck to me with unbearable closeness.
syn: nuisance; pest

4. **humility** (hyōō mil´ i tē) *n.* absence of vanity; humbleness
Even though Jo is a celebrated author, she's the picture of *humility* and never brags.
syn: modesty   *ant: vanity; arrogance*

5. **dolorous** (dō´ lə rəs) *adj.* exhibiting sorrow or pain
The song was so *dolorous* that Laura found it difficult not to cry.
syn: mournful   *ant: joyous*

6. **gargantuan** (gär gan´ chōō ən) *adj.* of huge or extraordinary size and power
Milltown's players were *gargantuan* compared with the small guys on our team.
syn: gigantic; huge   *ant: tiny*

7. **arduous** (är´ jōō əs) *adj.* difficult; requiring much effort
Refinishing the old bookcase proved an *arduous* task, but the results were well worth it.
syn: strenuous; laborious   *ant: easy; unchallenging*

8. **affable** (af´ ə bel) *adj.* friendly; agreeable; easy to talk to
The *affable* old man never lacked for visitors.
syn: amiable; good-natured   *ant: disagreeable; irascible*

9. **grandiloquent** (gran dil´ ə kwent) *adj.* pompous or high-flown in speech
Marcus gets *grandiloquent* when speaking of the theatre, assuming no one knows as much or has as refined a taste as he.
syn: pretentious   *ant: plain-spoken*

10. **agrarian** (ə grâr´ ē ən) *adj.* concerning farms, farmers, or
     the use of land
     The economy of the *agrarian* nation depended on good crop yields.
     syn: agricultural   *ant: urban; industrial*

11. **grimace** (grim´ is) *n.* a facial expression of fear, disapproval, or pain
     Amanda gave a *grimace* when Mrs. Hind assigned nine pages of algebra
     homework.
     syn: scowl   *ant: smile*

12. **harangue** (hə rang´) *n.* a long, strongly expressed speech or lecture
     My wife delivered a lengthy *harangue* this morning in an effort to get me
     to quit smoking.
     syn: tirade

13. **formidable** (fôr´ mi də bəl) *adj.* arousing fear or awe
     When the hulking, 250-lb man stepped into the ring, Oscar knew that he
     had to face a *formidable* opponent.
     syn: intimidating

14. **sycophant** (sik´ ə fənt) n. a flatterer; one who fawns on others in
     order to gain favor
     Teri was such a *sycophant* that she always laughed loudly at her
     supervisor's awful jokes.
     syn: toady   *ant: contrarian*

15. **explicit** (ik splis´ ît) *adj.* clearly and openly stated; leaving nothing to
     the imagination
     Mom's instructions were *explicit*: Do not leave the house for any reason.
     syn: exact; precise   *ant: ambiguous; vague*

Exercise I

Words in Context

From the list below, supply the words needed to complete the paragraph. Some words will not be used.

gadfly	humility	arduous	affable
grandiloquent	harangue	grimace	sycophant
explicit	agrarian		

A.　"All the king's horses and all the king's men showed up tonight!" mused Wyston to himself as he snatched another glass of champagne from the server's tray. He hated the governor's cocktail parties; it was always a[n] _____ task to maintain a friendly, _____ demeanor around so many obvious _____ seeking favors from the administration. After two hours, Wyston had to struggle to prevent his tired, polite smile from turning into a _____. It took all he had to pretend to listen and nod at the _____ stories of the "wannabe rich and famous." There was also the annoying babble of the _____—single attendees who lacked the _____ required to be seen alone. They forced themselves into conversations and then held the listeners captive by withholding any opportunities to escape. When Wyston could no longer tolerate the pestering, he stepped outside and waited for the Governor to arrive and deliver his _____ to the idiotic crowd.

From the list below, supply the words needed to complete the paragraph. Some words will not be used.

humility	dolorous	agrarian	gadfly	gargantuan
avid	explicit	formidable	epistle	

B.　The atmosphere at Aunt Agnes's farmhouse was _____ during the wake following the funeral. No one could believe that Agnes was gone. At least, they reasoned, the _____ equestrian died while doing something that she loved. There was no definite explanation as to why Agnes's horse bucked her off, but by the looks of the _____ animal tracks, the horse had been spooked by a[n] _____ wolf, perhaps the largest ever seen.

　　The threat of wolves was nothing new to the _____ Van Ness family, who had been farming the northern valley for six generations. Wolves had attacked horses on the farm in the past, especially during extremely cold winters such as this one. Children on the farm always had _____ instructions to stay within sight of the house, but sometimes not even that was enough to protect the family from the hungry, silver predators.

　　Vicky, a niece, wandered up the stairway to the second floor. Memories of her youth flashed through her head as she entered Agnes's, and sat on the corner of the bed, and noticed the dusty corner of an old shoebox protruding from beneath the vanity. Curious, Vicky retrieved the box and, to her surprise, she found thirty years of hand-written _____, some of which were for Agnes, and some of which Agnes wrote but never sent.

Exercise II

Sentence Completion

Complete the sentence in a way that shows you understand the meaning of the italicized vocabulary word.

1. The summer help on the highway crew underestimated the *arduous* task of...

2. Through the smoke, I could tell by the *grimace* on Danforth's face that he...

3. Elliot could hardly tolerate the *grandiloquent* aristocrats while working at the...

4. To the dismay of the *sycophants*, the new foreman...

5. Jamie, the annoying *gadfly*, has a habit of...

6. The beach town published *explicit* rules about...

7. The arrogant stockbroker learned *humility* after...

8. In *agrarian* states, many young adults have extensive knowledge of...

9. The *gargantuan* Kodiak bear devoured...

10. Needing a break from her *dolorous* work as a coroner, Dr. Sinclair...

11. Unlike the fox, the bear turned out to be a *formidable* opponent because...

12. The history teacher's *harangue* this morning seemed to...

13. Mary Ellen's *avid* interest in chemistry led to her career as...

14. The senator's biography was actually a collection of *epistles* that...

15. The *affable* receptionist made everyone feel...

Exercise III

Roots, Prefixes, and Suffixes

Study the entries and answer the questions that follow.

The root *cosm* means "world" or "universe."
The root *cred* means "believe."
The suffixes *ic* and *id* mean "of" or "like."

A. *Using literal translations as guidance, define the following words without using a dictionary:*
   1. cosmic
   2. cosmos
   3. credible
   4. creed
   5. credentials
   6. credence

B. *Micro* means "small"; therefore, the word *microcosm* refers to a[n] _____ _____.

C. *Polites* means "citizen"; therefore, a *cosmopolitan* person is _____ _____.

D. List as many words as you can think of that contain the root *cred*.

Exercise IV

Inference

Complete the sentences by inferring information about the italicized word from its context.

A. If Kevin is no longer *affable* after his meeting with the manager, we might assume that the manager…

B. After the hard tackle during the championship game, the coach saw the *grimace* on Todd's face and knew…

C. Everyone knew that Bonnie was a *sycophant* because whenever the governor entered the room, Bonnie would…

Exercise V

Writing

Here is a writing prompt similar to the one you will find on the essay writing portion of the ACT.

> When schools face budget cuts, which programs should be the first to go, and why? Extracurricular activities, of course, are typically the first programs to be terminated, but should that be the case? Should sports and music programs have a lower priority than other parts of the curriculum (other than the core curriculum of math, science, and English)?
>
> Write a letter to a school board and suggest which programs, types of programs, or parts of the curriculum should be the first to be cut. Think of at least three candidates for termination, and explain in detail why each one should not be spared. Consider the ultimate benefit of the programs to the education of the students.

Thesis: Write a *one-sentence* response to the above assignment. Make certain this single sentence offers a clear statement of your position.

Example: For students who are not natural academics, sports and music are as important to development as calculus or literature and should be spared from budget cuts.

_____

_____

Organizational Plan: List at least three subtopics you will use to support your main idea. This list is your outline.

1. _____

2. _____

3. _____

Draft: Following your outline, write a good first draft of your essay. Remember to support all your points with examples, facts, references to reading, etc.

Review and Revise: Exchange essays with a classmate. Using the scoring guide for Organization on page 224, score your partner's essay (while he or she scores yours). Focus on the organizational plan and use of language conventions. If necessary, rewrite your essay to improve the organizational plan and the use of language.

Exercise VI

English Practice

Improving Paragraphs
Read the following passage and then choose the best revision for the underlined portions of the paragraph. The questions will require you to make decisions regarding the revision of the reading selection. Some revisions are not of actual mistakes, but will improve the clarity of the writing.

D-Day

[1]

On November 8, 1942, American soldiers landed in North Africa. Fighting alongside the British Eighth Army, the Americans pushed the Germans out of North Africa. When the campaign was over, on May 12, 1943, the Allies had lost 70,000 men,[1] while killing, wounding and capturing 350,000 Italian and German (Axis) soldiers. With North Africa taken, the Allies then invaded Italy. The plan was to drive up the boot of Italy, right into Germany, or so it seemed. Meanwhile, however,[2] Allied plans to invade the continent of Europe on the French coast were moving forward.

1. A. NO CHANGE
   B. When the campaign was over, the Allies had lost 70,000 men, on May 12, 1943,
   C. When the campaign was over —May 12, 1943,—the Allies had lost 70,000 men,
   D. On May 12, 1943, when the campaign was over, the Allies had lost 70,000 men

2. Which of the following would best improve the last two sentences of the first paragraph?
   F. The plan, it seemed, was to drive up the boot of Italy, right into Germany; meanwhile, however,
   G. The plan was to drive up the boot of Italy, right into Germany, or so it seemed. Meanwhile:
   H. the plan was to drive up the boot of Italy, right into Germany. Meanwhile, however,
   J. The plan, so it seemed, was to drive up the boot of Italy, right into Germany. But,

[2]

The German generals, pessimistic at this point in the war, had good reason <u>to be pessimistic</u>.[3] They were pressed on the Eastern front by the Russians and in Italy by the Allies. Additionally, the German generals had an entire continent on which a third battlefront would surely be opened. Hitler and his generals knew that the pending Allied invasion would have to be crushed quickly. Only in this way could Hitler send more men to halt the Russian advance in the <u>East.</u> <u>It was in this mood</u>[4] Hitler named General Rommel to be in charge of coastal defenses in France. While Hitler blamed Rommel for the defeats in North Africa, <u>he also knew that he was the most brilliant general he had.</u>[5]

3. A. NO CHANGE
   B. to be overly pessimistic
   C. to be
   D. to be that way

4. A. NO CHANGE
   B. East; consequently,
   C. East. Because of that,
   D. East and since he was in
      that mood,

5. A. NO CHANGE
   B. he also knew that he was
      the most brilliant general
      Hitler had.
   C. Hitler also knew that
      Rommel was the most
      brilliant general he had.
   D. Rommel also knew that
      he was the most brilliant
      general Hitler had

[3]

When Rommel arrived, he was amazed at how little defensive work had been done. <u>Throwing himself into his work, construction was begun by Rommel on what he called the Atlantic Wall.</u>[6] This was to be a wall of coastal defenses that stretched from Norway to Spain. If <u>Rommel had had</u> the benefit of a few more months, some observers think he might have affected the outcome of the invasion. Another problem was the confusion in the German general staff.[8] Because no one on the scene had complete authority, important things frequently did not get done. If Rommel had been in complete charge, some experts think that the Allied invasion would have been in more greater trouble.

6. F. NO CHANGE
   G. Throwing himself into his work, construction was begun on what, Rommel called the Atlantic Wall.
   H. Having thrown himself into his work, Rommel built the Atlantic Wall.
   J. Throwing himself into his work, Rommel began construction on what he called the Atlantic Wall.

7. A. NO CHANGE
   B. has had
   C. had
   D. would have had

[4]

On June 6, 1944, the invasion <u>began, more than</u>[8] 150,000 Allied troops landed on the beaches. They came ashore on the northern coast of France at Normandy. Their mission was to push Hitler's army back across the continent and completely crush the Nazi war machine. The soldiers were mostly from Britain, Canada, and the United States. The landing force had been preceded by 13,000 paratroopers who dropped behind the enemy's lines. The total invasion force <u>were</u>[9] backed by the full force of Allied sea and air power. In the air, the Allies enjoyed a fifty-to-one advantage. On the ground they conducted the biggest amphibious assault ever attempted in modern warfare. Equipment for this landing had been stockpiled in England in the months before the invasion. Code <u>named "*Operation Overlord.*"</u>[10] it was more popularly known as "D-Day." This attack proved to be the beginning of the end for Hitler and Nazi Germany.

8. F. NO CHANGE
   G. began. More than
   H. began; more than
   J. began with

9. A. NO CHANGE
   B. was
   C. were to be
   D. was to be

10. F. NO CHANGE
    G. named, "*Operation Overlord,*"
    H. named "Operation Overlord",
    J. named "Operation Overlord,"

[5]

U.S. General Dwight Eisenhower was the Supreme Commander of Allied forces based in Britain. He had the responsibility for leading the attack on the European continent. Eisenhower had described the military power that waited for D-Day as "a coiled spring." It was his responsibility to pick the day on which this "coiled spring" would let loose. <u>In other words he must make the decision on when to launch the attack</u>.[11] This was a massive responsibility, and the bad weather in the English Channel made it a tortuous decision. There had already been two delays because of the weather. On June 6, <u>however,</u>[12] Eisenhower gave the signal for the invasion to begin. The timing could not have been better. A brief break in the rainy weather that day allowed the ships to land the men and the tanks. <u>Also, in addition,</u>[13] Field Marshall Rommel had been convinced that the gale-force winds would continue. Knowing that the Allies had a history of waiting for clear weather, Rommel had decided that it was safe to return to Germany for his wife's birthday party. By the time he got back to the battlefront, the Allies were firmly dug in on French soil. The Allies had gotten a foothold on the continent, and they would not be turned back.

11. What should be done with the sentence in paragraph 5 that begins, *In other words* and ends with *attack?*
   A. Shorten it.
   B. Delete it.
   C. Lengthen it.
   D. Move it.

12. F. NO CHANGE
   G. therefore,
   H. however;
   J. on the other hand,

13. A. NO CHANGE
   B. In addition,
   C. Also, additionally,
   D. Also

[6]

In planning the invasion, <u>fooling the enemy about the landing places was known by Eisenhower to be very important</u>.[14] In a brilliant plan of deception, Eisenhower had created a phony military unit called FUSAG or the First United States Army Group. Information was intentionally leaked to the Germans that this was the invading force that would land at Calais, France. Fake messages were sent, false troop locations were reported, and metal strips were dropped from planes to give the appearance of large air squadrons on German radar. This scheme was so convincing that Hitler was still waiting for the assault on Calais six weeks after the Allies landed at Normandy. <u>The months following the assault on Normandy would see the Axis powers in full retreat on all fronts.</u>[15]

14. F. NO CHANGE
   G. Eisenhower knew that it was very important to confuse the enemy as to which of the landing places the Allies were going to use to invade.
   H. it was known by Eisenhower that fooling the enemy about the landing places was very important
   J. Eisenhower knew that fooling the enemy about the landing places was very important

15. How could the last sentence of the essay be improved?
   A NO CHANGE
   B. Reemphasize the success of the FUSAG ruse.
   C. Delete it entirely.
   D. Use it as the topic sentence of a new concluding paragraph.

Vocabulary
Power Plus
for the
ACT
Vocabulary,
Reading, and Writing
Exercises for High Scores

Book Two

Lesson Twelve

1. **altercation** (ôl tər kā´ shən) *n.* a heated argument
    The mounting tension finally spawned an *altercation* between the police
    and the residents.
    syn: quarrel; dispute   *ant: agreement; harmony*

2. **lexicon** (lek´ si kon´) *n.* a dictionary; a specialized vocabulary
    used in a particular field or place
    Having grown up in the inner city, Shawn was familiar with the
    lexicon of the streets.
    syn: jargon; argot; cant

3. **hue** (hyōō) *n.* a particular shade of a given color
    Dad was going to paint the shutters magenta, but Mom hates that
    hue and nixed the idea.

4. **galvanize** (gal´ və nīz) *v.* to startle into sudden activity
    A slight motion of the guard's rifle *galvanized* the lazy work crew
    into action.
    syn: stimulate   *ant: enervate*

5. **sanction** (sangk´ shən) *n.* permission; support
    The teacher gave *sanction* to the student's odd but harmless habit
    of doing his homework in crayon.

6. **hyperbole** (hī pûr´ bə lē) *n.* extreme exaggeration for effect and not
    meant to be taken literally
    When Susan told her son she was going to kill him, it was only *hyperbole*.
    ant: understatement

7. **ominous** (om´ ə nəs) *adj.* threatening; foreboding evil
    We went on our picnic despite the *ominous* rain clouds.
    syn: sinister   *ant: comforting*

8. **audacity** (ô das´ i tē) *n.* rude boldness; nerve
    Kate's father was enraged when she had the *audacity* to talk back to him.
    syn: insolence; impudence   *ant: decorum*

9. **evince** (i vins´) *v.* to demonstrate clearly; to prove
   If you *evince* your theory, the university will fund your further studies.
   syn: manifest

10. **implacable** (im pla´ kə bəl) *adj.* unable to be appeased or pacified
    Her *implacable* suspicions were finally put to rest when a private investigator
    assured her that her husband was faithful.
    syn: inflexible; relentless   *ant: pacified; assuaged*

11. **exhort** (ig zôrt´) *v.* to urge on with stirring words
    During halftime, the coach *exhorted* his team to "win one for the Gipper."
    syn: encourage

12. **incarcerate** (in kär´ sə rāt) *v.* to put into prison; to confine
    We were shocked that the police *incarcerated* Rafael for something as minor
    as stealing hubcaps.
    syn: imprison; constrain   *ant: liberate; free*

13. **incisive** (in sī´ siv) *adj.* sharp; keen; cutting straight to the heart of the
    matter
    I had thought the meeting would run for hours, but Sharon made a few
    incisive comments that settled matters without wasting time or words.
    syn: piercing; acute   *ant: superficial; dull*

14. **expedient** (ik spē´ dē ənt) *adj.* practical; providing an immediate
    advantage (especially when serving one's self-interest)
    Lying, while not admirable, did prove to be the most *expedient* way to
    obtain the information.
    syn: effective   *ant: feckless*

15. **pertinent** (pûr´ tn ənt) *adj.* having to do with the subject at hand;
    relevant
    The lecturer took questions as long as they were *pertinent* and enriched the
    discussion.
                                                     ant: unrelated; extraneous

Exercise I

Words in Context

From the list below, supply the words needed to complete the paragraph. Some words will not be used.

ominous	exhort	galvanize	hyperbole
expedient	implacable	incisive	hue

A.   "What are you doing, you guys? I shouldn't have to _____ you at this point in the game!" _____ by Liza's scream, the four workers picked up their sanders and returned to their unfinished portions of drywall.

"We're two days overdue! That means we're paying them now!" The worker closest to Liza turned a[n] _____ of red as she screamed. He knew that Liza's lecture was not merely _____ to get the team to work faster; the contractors really were beyond their deadline. Liza was worried for good reason; if the company couldn't prove that it was capable of _____, short-notice refurbishing, it would more than likely lose its contract with the city.

Myron, the site foreman, appreciated Liza's _____ comments. At least she took the time to explain why the workers needed to labor more quickly. Such practice reminded the workers of just how small the degree of separation was between the company's success and their paychecks. It also prevented the workers from classifying Liza as a[n] _____ manager who just wanted to make a profit. If the workers knew that the company was suffering, they knew that their jobs were in jeopardy.

From the list below, supply the words needed to complete the paragraph. Some words will not be used.

altercation	lexicon	sanction	ominous
audacity	evince	incarcerate	pertinent
implacable	galvanize		

B. Eugene had worked at the genetics lab for six days when he witnessed the noisy _____ between Dr. Strangeon and his research assistant.
"You know that I didn't _____ an early run of the cloning module! Now you've destroyed the entire lot!" Strangeon was definitely irate, and Eugene wished that he understood more of the laboratory _____ that the doctor spouted at his assistant.

"How could you—you're not an intern anymore—how could you have the _____ to go off on your own and initiate a test run of a model that required eight years of research and over twelve million dollars to develop? Well?" The assistant could only mutter an answer.

"I just thought—I—uh—I wanted to see if—"

"What you want is not _____ here!" shouted the doctor. "You've only managed to _____ the fact that you're unfit to work in a laboratory! We should press charges and have the police _____ you! Now get out!"

The problem, thought Eugene, probably involved whatever Dr. Strangeon stored behind the _____ pair of tall, armored doors with the retina-scanning lock mechanism. Dr. Strangeon and his assistant had been the only two people to enter that room during the week that Eugene had been employed at the lab.

Exercise II

Sentence Completion

Complete the sentence in a way that shows you understand the meaning of the italicized vocabulary word.

1. The *ominous* gates in front of the old mansion made us...

2. Lonnie's face turned a sickly *hue* of green after...

3. Be sure to get *sanction* before you try to enter the...

4. The *incisive* instructions made it easy for Lynn to...

5. The *expedience* the town showed in building a dam of sandbags...

6. *Galvanized* by the sound of the screaming foreman, the workers...

7. In the courtroom, the prisoner had the *audacity* to...

8. I don't need to *evince* my value at this company because...

9. During the peace talks, the *implacable* general refused...

10. The physical *altercation* between the brothers caused the neighbors to...

11. The sergeant was advised to *exhort* the platoon prior to the...

12. To master the *lexicon* of the law, John...

13. It seemed *hyperbole* to me when my teacher said...

14. The paramedics wanted only *pertinent* information because...

15. The judge decided to *incarcerate* Tara because...

Exercise III

Roots, Prefixes, and Suffixes

Study the entries and answer the questions that follow.

The root *dorm* means "sleep."
The root *fin* means "end."
The suffix *ory* means "a place for."
The root *nom* means "name."
The suffix *ee* means "one who is."
The prefix *in* means "not."
The root *clat* means "calling" or "system of calling."

A. *Using literal translations as guidance, define the following words without using a dictionary:*

1. dormitory
2. dormant
3. nominee
4. nomenclature
5. finale
6. infinite

B. You might see the grand finale at the _____ of a show.

C. Since the mayor-for-a-day position was only *nominal*, Colette could not

_____.

D. List as many words as you can think of that contain the roots *dorm, fin,* and *nom.*

Exercise IV

Inference

Complete the sentences by inferring information about the italicized word from its context.

A. If you don't have *sanction* to sell refreshments in the stadium, the security guards might...

B. Mr. Moulan's *expedient* methods to get rich were probably to blame for...

C. Judging by the debris on the highway and the intensity of the drivers' *altercation*, I assumed that the two drivers...

Exercise V

Critical Reading

Below is a reading passage followed by several multiple-choice questions similar to the ones you will encounter on the ACT. Carefully read the passage and choose the best answer to each of the questions.

Over three hundred years ago, Alexander Pope wrote, in an essay, "A little learning is a dangerous thing." Pope's statement is a truth for every time and place, even among the most learned people in civilization.

Little Boy and *Fat Man*, the only two atomic bombs to be used offensively in the
5   history of the world, ended the war with Japan in 1945 and thrust the world into the atomic age. The awesome and terrible power of these first fission bombs was the product of the most massive secret project in all of warfare: the Manhattan Project. The project involved more than 120,000 people, including some of the brightest scientists of the century—mathematicians and nuclear physicists from several
10   nations.

Nuclear weapons and energy research became the top priority after the end of the war, and the veteran scientists of the Manhattan Project passed on knowledge to the next generation of nuclear scientists. Despite cutting edge advancements in atomic engineering and theory, however, safety was often an afterthought amid the
15   exciting potential of this yet-unexploited resource. The first generation of nuclear scientists were truly pioneers, and the regions they explored were full of dangers that were known, perhaps, but hadn't been experienced often enough to cause fear.

Substances that spontaneously undergo nuclear fission are called fissile materials, with the most well-known being enriched uranium and plutonium. As
20   the atoms of a fissile substance decay, they radiate (among other particles) neutrons. Each neutron radiated has the potential to split another atom of the substance, and so on, with each split releasing energy and another neutron. If there is enough fissile material arranged in just the right way, each free neutron will go on to split another atom and so forth, causing a chain reaction, or critical assembly.

25   Looking back at the origin of atomic weapons research makes it easier to understand how fatal incidents could occur in the name of science, albeit in controlled laboratory or classroom situations. The first nuclear reactor was little more than a pile of uranium dioxide perforated with cadmium control rods (rods that absorb neutrons and thus allow the operator to control the fission). While
30   the experiment sounds mild, know that researchers constructed the unshielded, uncooled stack of fissile uranium, aptly named *Chicago Pile-1*, beneath the bleachers of a stadium at the University of Chicago—in the middle of a city! Their safety procedure? A man stood at ready with an axe, waiting to sever the rope suspending the control rods above the pile, should the operators lose control of the chain
35   reaction.

In 1945, Harry Daghlian, a nuclear physicist, was conducting experiments on a plutonium sphere about the size of an orange—a subcritical mass, or an amount of

plutonium not large enough to sustain a nuclear chain reaction on its own. Daghlian
accidentally dropped a tungsten carbide brick on the sphere. Tungsten functions
40 like a mirror for neutrons, reflecting them back into the mass of plutonium where
they split more atoms. The condition caused a critical mass, and from the plutonium
came a fatal dose of radiation that killed Daghlian in less than a month.

The very same plutonium sphere that killed Daghlian remained in use at
Los Alamos, in spite of its history; one must remember that the effort to isolate
45 plutonium was so costly ($2 billion) that the value of plutonium was tens of
thousands of dollars per gram. In 1946, just nine months after the demon core
killed Daghlian, a physicist named Louis Slotin used the sphere to conduct critical
mass experiments in a room with seven observers, slowly lowering a beryllium
hemisphere onto the demon core with only the tip of a screwdriver preventing the
50 masses from getting too close together, known also as "tickling the dragon's tail."
Because beryllium, like tungsten oxide, is a neutron reflector, it caused the demon
core to approach critical mass as Slotin lowered it.

An eerie blue flash illuminated the room and observers reported feeling a wave
of heat when the beryllium slipped from Slotin's grasp and closed upon the demon
55 core. Quickly, Slotin snatched the beryllium away from the critical assembly,
stopping the fission—but the damage had already been done. Slotin suffered
for nine days before succumbing to the massive dose of radiation. Slotin's body
absorbed the bulk of the radiation; though the nearest man was hospitalized, Slotin
alone received a lethal dose.

60 To say that Daghlian or Slotin or any of the pioneer physicists suffered from "a
little learning" would, of course, be the worst type of disinformation; these scientists
probably forgot more nuclear physics knowledge in a week than the average person
acquires in a lifetime. Slotin, though only 35 years of age at his death, constructed
the Trinity test bomb—the first atomic bomb in the history of mankind. The main
65 oversight in the early atomic age was, perhaps, complacency—not ignorance. The
science was so new that experience had not yet provided the examples that prompt
the necessary vigilance; lab casualties had been few in spite of the frequent taunting
of the nuclear dragon. Scientists were researching and working with materials that
had the potential to end wars and provide electricity to the world; the excitement
70 of the time was immeasurable—it was a crossroads in history and a celebration of
human ingenuity.

1. The tone of the passage could best be described as
   A. reverent.
   B. scathing.
   C. accurate.
   D. admiring.

2. According to the passage, the particle that is central to sustaining fission is
   called a(n)
   F. alpha.
   G. tritium.
   H. neutron.
   J. electron.

3. The item referred to as the "demon core" is
   A. the plutonium instrumental in the deaths of two scientists.
   B. the cadmium control rod used to slow fission in Chicago Pile 1.
   C. the beryllium neutron reflector used to create a critical assembly.
   D. the fissile uranium used to build the Trinity bomb.

4. The quotation in the introduction is analogous to the phrase,
   F. the first generation of atomic scientists were cowboys.
   G. research must never impede hands-on experiments.
   H. performing research without enough data is foolish.
   J. there is such a thing as too much knowledge.

5. The author's attitude toward the development of nuclear technology is best described as
   A. supportive.
   B. skeptical.
   C. apologetic.
   D. accusatory.

6. Which of the following situations would NOT be an example of "tickling the dragon's tail"? (line 50)
   F. teasing a dog known to bite people
   G. watching television for eight hours straight
   H. investing a large amount of money with a stranger
   J. walking on a frozen, snow-covered lake in the spring

7. What is the most likely reason for the misleading project and device names?
   A. The research project was mired in confusing government bureaucracy.
   B. The Chicago Pile reactor was built in Manhattan.
   C. The names were to mislead spies and keep the projects secret.
   D. The projects were named for the locations of the laboratories.

8. Choose the answer that best describes the organization of the essay:
   F. increasing importance
   G. chronological
   H. cause and effect
   J. compare and contrast

9. The most probable intent of the passage is
    A. to dissuade the further development of nuclear technology.
    B. to inform about the risks and sacrifices of new technologies.
    C. to apologize for the use of atomic bombs.
    D. to solicit more attention to nuclear research.

10. Of the following choices, which is the most suitable title for this passage?
    F. Atomic Age Madmen
    G. The Dawn of Nuclear Energy
    H. Slotin's Sacrifice
    J. Tickling the Dragon's Tail

Book Two

Lesson Thirteen

1. **inert** (in ûrt´) *adj.* unable to act or move; inactive; sluggish
   All dangerous components have been removed from the *inert* missile on display at the science museum.
   syn: dormant; passive   *ant: dynamic; active*

2. **circumvent** (sûr kəm vent´) *v.* to get around; to bypass
   Though she did not lie, the defendant *circumvented* the question by claiming she could not remember where she was at the time.
   syn: avoid

3. **clandestine** (klan des´ tin) *adj.* secret
   Romeo and Juliet were forced to hold *clandestine* meetings because of their parents' feuding.
   syn: covert; furtive   *ant: open; aboveboard*

4. **acquit** (ə kwit´) *v.* to find not guilty of a fault or crime
   The jury *acquitted* the man, and he was free to go.
   syn: absolve   *ant: convict*

5. **deprecate** (dep´ ri kāt) *v.* to express strong disapproval of
   Doug stopped offering new ideas after the other workers *deprecated* his first suggestion.
   syn: deplore   *ant: approve; praise*

6. **barrister** (bar´ i stər) *n.* lawyer (British)
   The *barrister* questioned the witness as to his familiarity with a certain London pub.

7. **adulation** (aj ōō lā´ shən) *n.* excessive praise or admiration
   Kim despised the *adulation* heaped on rock stars by young fans.
   syn: flattery; adoration   *ant: derision*

8. **culinary** (kul´ ə ner ē) *adj.* having to do with the kitchen or cooking
   The famous chef had been a life-long student of the *culinary* arts.

9. **bawdy** (bô´ dē) *adj.* indecent; humorously obscene
   When some called the new sitcom *bawdy*, the toy company quickly withdrew its sponsorship.
   syn: risqué; lewd   *ant: innocent; clean*

10. **chastise** (chas tīz´) *v.* to punish severely
Professor Jacques *chastised* Archie for skipping Latin and gave him ten extra chapters to translate.
syn: discipline

11. **jocose** (jō kōs´) *adj.* joking; humorous
Gary's *jocose* manner often led people to say he should become a stand-up comedian.
syn: witty; funny; playful; jocund   *ant: serious*

12. **myriad** (mir´ ē əd) *n.* a very large number
                              adj. too numerous to be counted
    (n.) After my break-up, my mom fed me the old line about there being a *myriad* of fish in the sea.
    (a.) The biologist spent her entire career categorizing the *myriad* plant species of the rain forest.
    (n.) *syn: host; multitude*
    (a.) *syn: countless; innumerable*   *ant: few; limited*

13. **latent** (lāt´ nt) *adj.* present, but not active; hidden
After retiring, Nat took up painting and found that he had had *latent* artistic talents all along.
syn: dormant   *ant: manifest*

14. **pernicious** (pər nish´ əs) *adj.* destructive; deadly
The *pernicious* plague wiped out half the country's population.
syn: malignant; harmful   *ant: benign*

15. **frugal** (frōō´ gəl) *adj.* thrifty; economical in money matters
My *frugal* father buys only day-old bread and marked-down fruit.
syn: economical   *ant: wasteful; profligate*

Exercise I

Words in Context

From the list below, supply the words needed to complete the paragraph. Some words will not be used.

culinary	pernicious	latent	frugal	circumvent
clandestine	inert	jocose	myriad	

A. Like a[n] _____ saboteur hiding in enemy territory waiting for the go-ahead signal, the tiny microorganism infiltrated the deepest, most vulnerable parts of its host and remained in a dormant state. Waves of red blood cells knocked the _____ bacterium about, tossing its _____, suspended form from one membrane to the next. The germ waited, as it had for days, until the host's chemistry was perfect for waking from its slumber and unleashing its _____ poison in the host's body. In a few hours, the single microbe would multiply into _____ bundles of destruction, and then the tiny legion would seize control of the host's nervous system. Not even the best research scientists could find a way to _____ the deadly effects of the microscopic villains.

From the list below, supply the words needed to complete the paragraph. Some words will not be used.

adulation	frugal	acquit	myriad
jocose	barrister	chastise	deprecate

B. "What are you being so _____ about? We're in a courtroom, you fool; shut up."

Scolded by his only friend in the room, Giles stopped laughing but maintained his crooked smirk. His _____ was quickly losing patience; both he and Giles knew that there was no chance that the judge was going to _____ him. This was his second appearance before Justice Quentin, and by the way in which the judge _____ Giles during the previous trial, he knew that he wasn't going to get away this time. As the smirk faded, Giles wished that he hadn't been so _____ while shopping for lawyers.

From the list below, supply the words needed to complete the paragraph. Some words will not be used.

frugal   bawdy   adulation   clandestine   deprecate   culinary

C.   Theme restaurants do not usually become popular for the quality of their cuisine, but the Gold Mine, operated in the likeness of a California gold-rush saloon, has received the _____ of every food critic who ate there. The saloon is one of few tourism-dependent restaurants that gives as much attention to its _____ performance as to the nightly stage shows featuring vaudeville-style comedians, singers, and cancan dancers wearing the _____ saloon outfits of the period. After twenty years of service, few patrons—if any—have been able to _____ the quality of food and entertainment at the Gold Mine.

Exercise II

Sentence Completion

Complete the sentence in a way that shows you understand the meaning of the italicized vocabulary word.

1.   Pete was *acquitted* of the crime, but the general public still believed...

2.   My *bawdy* uncle really didn't fit in at the...

3.   As the fallen disco ball struck the floor, a *myriad* of...

4.   Richard was so *frugal* that he refused to...

5.   To sneak the missile data out of the compound, the *clandestine* operator...

6.   The *barrister* feared his client's associates after...

7.   The *latent* saboteur waited for the signal to...

8.   The swarm of *pernicious* locusts caused the farmer to...

9.   No one thought that it was too extreme to *chastise* Gary for...

10.   The crowd's *adulation* for Monique revealed her...

11. When you finish using the *culinary* utensils, please...

12. Some people laugh at Ken, but others find his *jocose* manner to be...

13. Feel free to *deprecate* my idea now, but not when we're in front of...

14. The *inert* Jose lay on the couch after an exhausting day of...

15. To *circumvent* the broken power line, the electric company...

Exercise III

Roots, Prefixes, and Suffixes

Study the entries and answer the questions that follow.

> The roots *fac, fact, fect,* and *fic* mean "make" or "do."
> The root *grat* means "please."
> The suffix *tude* means "the state of."
> The roots *mot* and *mov* mean "to move."
> The prefix *con* means "with."
> The prefix *re* means "away."
> The prefix *de* means "down."

A. *Using literal translations as guidance, define the following words without using a dictionary:*

   1. factory
   2. gratitude
   3. congratulations
   4. motivation
   5. remote
   6. demote

B. A person who does certain activities very well can be said to have a _____ for them.
   If you ease the progress of a class meeting, you could be called a[n] _____.

C. If you are feeling thankful for someone's help, you might describe your feeling as _____.

D. List as many words as you can think of that contain the roots *fac, fact, fect, fic,* or *grat*.

Exercise IV

Inference

Complete the sentences by inferring information about the italicized word from its context.

A. If the foreman usually *deprecates* the behavior of his employees, the workers will probably...

B. If Eddie's parents *chastise* him by taking away his car keys, you might assume that Eddie...

C. When a *myriad* of sparks emerged from beneath her car, Lanna was glad that she...

Exercise V

Writing

Here is a writing prompt similar to the one you will find on the essay writing portion of the ACT.

> Has physical education in school become obsolete or unnecessary? Schools are beginning to allow students to opt out of gym class, to either the delight or disdain of students and parents. Some schools will waive PE if students are enrolled in other physical activities such as sports, cheerleading, or marching band.
>
> Should waivers become the norm for American schools, or is PE valuable enough to keep in the curriculum, or perhaps even improve?
>
> Write a letter to the school board that details your case for or against physical education. Support your argument with at least three subtopics.

Thesis: Write a *one-sentence* response to the above assignment. Make certain this single sentence offers a clear statement of your position.

Example: Waivers will ensure that the students who most need exercise are not getting it, so schools should adopt a weekly half-day of gym class.

_____

_____

Organizational Plan: List at least three subtopics you will use to support your main idea. This list is your outline.

1. _____

2. _____

3. _____

Draft: Following your outline, write a good first draft of your essay. Remember to support all your points with examples, facts, references to reading, etc.

Review and Revise: Exchange essays with a classmate. Using the scoring guide for Development on page 225, score your partner's essay (while he or she scores yours). Focus on the development of ideas and use of language conventions. If necessary, rewrite your essay to improve the development and the use of language.

Exercise VI

English Practice

Identifying Sentence Errors
Identify the grammatical errors in the following sentences. If the sentence contains no error, select answer NO CHANGE.

1. All of the competitors knew which leg of the race <u>they were to run.</u>
   A. NO CHANGE
   B. he and she were to run.
   C. he or she were to run.
   D. they were running.

2. <u>Before the discovery of iron, there only were weapons made of bronze.</u>
   F. NO CHANGE
   G. Before the discovery of iron, only weapons were made of bronze.
   H. Before the discovery of iron, there were weapons made of bronze.
   J. Before the discovery of iron, weapons were made only of bronze.

3. Denny told the toll booth operator, "Hang on, I just dropped my <u>quarter".</u>
   A. NO CHANGE
   B. quarter."
   C. quarter.
   D. quarter"

4. The amazing magician, <u>who was beloved by audiences</u>, retired because of an uncontrollable quiver in his hands.
   F. NO CHANGE
   G. whom was beloved by audiences
   H. he who was beloved by audiences
   J. who audiences loved

5. Any woman who doesn't meet the necessary requirements will have <u>their name</u> removed from the list of candidates.
   A. NO CHANGE
   B. their title
   C. they're name
   D. her name

Improving Sentences

The underlined portion of each sentence contains some flaw. Select the answer that best corrects the flaw.

6. <u>Sleeping peacefully, we finally located the lost puppy in an abandoned mine tunnel.</u>
   - F. Sleeping peacefully, we located the puppy finally in an abandoned mine tunnel.
   - G. We finally located the lost puppy sleeping peacefully in an abandoned mine tunnel.
   - H. Finally, in an abandoned mine tunnel, we found the lost puppy.
   - J. We located the puppy in an abandoned mine sleeping peacefully.

7. The coach, along with the managers and team members, <u>were praised during the varsity sports banquet for an amazing performance that year.</u>
   - A. were praised for an amazing performance that year during the varsity sports banquet.
   - B. was praised during the varsity sports banquet for the year's amazing performance.
   - C. was praised for their year's amazing performance during their varsity sports banquet.
   - D. were praised for the year's amazing performance during the season.

8. <u>Our outdoor party quickly went inside when news of the approaching tornado was received by us.</u>
   - F. When our outdoor party went inside, we quickly heard news of an approaching tornado.
   - G. An approaching tornado was news, when our outdoor party went inside quickly.
   - H. Our outdoor party, when news of an approaching tornado went quickly, inside.
   - J. When we received news of an approaching tornado, our outdoor party quickly went inside.

9. <u>A suitcase was seen floating on Milltown Creek, but no one knew who's it was.</u>
   - A. A suitcase was seen floating on Milltown Creek, but no one knew whose it was.
   - B. No one knew whose suitcase was seen floating on Milltown Creek.
   - C. Floating on Milltown Creek was a suitcase, but no one knows whose it is.
   - D. Milltown Creek was seen with a floating suitcase, but no one knew who's it was.

10. <u>Finding a bag of sandwiches in the bank vault, while the police were investigating a bank robbery.</u>

    F. A bag of sandwiches was found in the bank while police were investigating the vault which was robbed.

    G. While they investigate a robbery, police were finding a bag of sandwiches in the bank vault.

    H. While investigating a bank robbery, police found a bag of sandwiches in the bank vault.

    J. The bank vault, a bag of sandwiches, and the police in a robbery investigation.

Book Two

Vocabulary
Power Plus
for the
ACT

Vocabulary,
Reading, and Writing
Exercises for High Scores

Lesson Fourteen

1. **levity** (lev´ i tē) *n.* lightness of disposition; lack of seriousness
   Kent brought an air of *levity* to the otherwise somber proceedings by cracking a few jokes.
   syn: frivolity   *ant: sobriety; somberness*

2. **hoax** (hōks) *n.* a practical joke; a trick
   The sighting of Elvis at the Bowl-O-Rama turned out to be a *hoax*.
   syn: fraud; fake

3. **amicable** (am´ i kə bəl) *adj.* friendly; peaceable
   Commerce will suffer until the two nations establish *amicable* relations.
   syn: agreeable; amiable   *ant: quarrelsome; warlike*

4. **obstreperous** (ob strep´ ər əs) *adj.* aggressively boisterous; stubborn and defiant
   The *obstreperous* demonstrators were forced to move by an icy blast from the fire hose.
                                                        ant: meek; tractable

5. **enraptured** (en rap´ chərd) *adj.* delighted beyond measure
   Sasha was *enraptured* by the performance of the visiting ballet troupe.
   syn: ecstatic

6. **marital** (mar´ i təl) *adj.* having to do with marriage
   Marital problems can sometimes be solved by a session with a marriage counselor.
   syn: wedded   *ant: single*

7. **bask** (bask) *v.* to expose oneself to pleasant warmth
   During the Florida vacation, all she did was *bask* in the sun.

8. **genial** (jēn´ yəl) *adj.* friendly; amiable
   Our new neighbors were so *genial* that we felt we had known them for years.
   syn: cordial   *ant: unfriendly*

9. **charlatan** (shär´ lə ten) *n.* one who pretends to have knowledge in order to swindle others
The supposed doctor endorsing the fat-burning "miracle drug" was actually a *charlatan*.
syn: quack; fraud   *ant: professional*

10. **mundane** (mun dān´) *adj.* commonplace; earthly and not spiritual
Virginia thought herself too good an artist to be expected to deal with *mundane* things like earning a living.
syn: boring   *ant: unique*

11. **fickle** (fik´ əl) *adj.* likely to change on a whim or without apparent reason
Because she never kept one boyfriend for long, her friends said Keisha was *fickle*.
syn: vacillating; capricious   *ant: steadfast*

12. **juggernaut** (jug´ ər nôt) *n.* a terrible destructive or irresistible force
The Nazi *juggernaut* swept through Belgium and into France.

13. **naïve** (nä ēv´) *adj.* simple in outlook; not affected or worldly; especially innocent
Old movies usually portray country girls in the city as *naïve* and vulnerable.
syn: unsophisticated; unsuspecting   *ant: sophisticated; cunning*

14. **nocturnal** (nok tûr´ nəl) *adj.* having to do with the night; occurring at night
Owls are *nocturnal* creatures; they sleep during the day.
       ant: diurnal

15. **novice** (nov´ is) *n.* a beginner; one who is inexperienced
The older lawyer took the *novice* under her wing and showed him the ropes.
syn: apprentice; tyro   *ant: master*

Exercise I

Words in Context

From the list below, supply the words needed to complete the paragraph. Some words will not be used.

charlatan	naïve	enraptured	hoax	amicable
levity	bask	fickle	mundane	

A.   When the _____ citizens of Reynoldsville finally realized that their forty-cent bottles of miracle sap contained nothing more than licorice extract and whiskey, they formed a lynch mob and searched for the _____ who had sold the fake elixir. unfortunately, Colonel Britton, the quack they were looking for, had already taken his wagon and quietly left town before dawn. He rode nonstop for a full day until, in his usual routine, he pulled far off the trail and spent a day restocking his miracle sap, occasionally breaking to partake of some himself. _____ by the beautiful scenery of the Black Hills, Britton didn't waste his opportunity to _____ in the low autumn sun for the remainder of the afternoon. While most of his clientele were desensitized to the beauty of nature after spending harsh lives in it, Britton never once considered his private outings to be _____; if he didn't spend at least a few hours enjoying nature every week, he had trouble maintaining his _____ demeanor whenever he rolled into a new town. If Britton didn't at least appear to be happy, people were not going to purchase his tonic, whether it was a[n] _____ or not. His customers were very _____ about spending their money; if they had even the slightest notion that Britton's product was a scam, they would not buy it.

From the list below, supply the words needed to complete the paragraph. Some words will not be used.

genial	enraptured	nocturnal	obstreperous
novice	juggernaut	marital	levity

B.   Despite her position as regional manager for Tyndall Systems, Shawna felt like a[n] _____ every time she attended the monthly sales meeting at Tyndall corporate headquarters. Perhaps she was just getting old, she reasoned, but she knew that few could endure her _____ schedule six days out of the week. Tyndall was a[n] _____ in the information technology arena, buying and consolidating other corporations and firing dissenters with impunity. Shawna told her husband that she would retire in two years; she hoped in time to mitigate their rapidly multiplying _____ problems. She was no longer the hard worker that Tyndall wanted for managing a regional hub, and the stress from trying to meet the demand had caused her once _____ manner to reverse—not that she needed it any more at the office. District sales meetings were not a place for _____; the twelve other managers spoke and carried themselves like assertive robots, rarely allowing jokes or laughter to interrupt their lengthy meetings. The single and most recent show of emotion at the meeting occurred when the vice president fired one of the managers on the spot, and the security guards had to drag him, _____ and screaming, out of the conference room.

Exercise II

Sentence Completion

Complete the sentence in a way that shows you understand the meaning of the italicized vocabulary word.

1. When the ambulance pulled up, everyone knew that Kristen's *hoax* had…

2. The *juggernaut* of tanks rolled effortlessly through…

3. The Clarks revealed few *marital* problems, but I knew that…

4. Katie *basked* in the bright August sun until she…

5. The *naïve* young soldier had difficulty accepting…

6. The *nocturnal* raccoons waited…

7. The zookeepers struggled to move the *obstreperous* lion to…

8. The *fickle* customers will not return to the store if…

9. Our *genial* neighbor always invites us…

10. Your *levity* in the present situation is…

11. No one ever would have guessed that the *charlatan* was not really a…

12. Mount Everest is not a place for *novice*…

13. The job might be *mundane*, but the city is…

14. Instead of attacking, the *amicable* natives…

15. Jules, an amateur chef, was *enraptured* by the master chef's invitation to…

Exercise III

Roots, Prefixes, and Suffixes

Study the entries, and answer the questions that follow.

The root *hydr* means "water."
The root *junct* means "join."
The suffix *phobia* means "fear of."
The prefix *de* means "down," "away from," "about."
The prefixes *dis*, *di*, and *dif* mean "apart" or "not."
The prefix *con* means "with."

A. *Using literal translations as guidance, define the following words without using a dictionary:*

1. dehydration
2. hydrophobia
3. disjointed
4. conjunction
5. juncture
6. hydroelectric

B. *Hydraulics* is the branch of physics that deals with _____ _____.

C. *Therm* is a root which means "heat"; therefore, *hydrothermal* has to do with _____.

D. List as many words as you can think of that contain the roots *hydr* and *junct*.

Exercise IV

Inference

Complete the sentences by inferring information about the italicized word from its context.

A. If the police determine that the suspicious package is a *hoax*, then it is probably safe for the evacuated employees to…

B. All the drivers waiting on the highway honked their horns because the farmer couldn't get the *obstreperous*…

C. If people respond to Myra's *levity* with angry glares, it is because she shouldn't be…

> ## Exercise V
> # *Critical Reading*

Below is a reading passage followed by several multiple-choice questions similar to the ones you will encounter on the ACT. Carefully read the passage and choose the best answer to each of the questions.

The following is an excerpt from Mark Twain's satirical essay, "On the Decay of the Art of Lying." Twain discusses the types of truth that people do—and do not—want to hear.

    Observe, I do not mean to suggest that the *custom* of lying has suffered any decay or interruption—no, for the Lie, as a Virtue, a Principle, is eternal; the Lie, as a recreation, a solace, a refuge in time of need, the fourth Grace, the tenth Muse, man's best and surest friend, is immortal, and cannot perish from the earth while
5 this club remains. My complaint simply concerns the decay of the *art* of lying. No high-minded man, no man of right feeling, can contemplate the lumbering and slovenly lying of the present day without grieving to see a noble art so prostituted. In this veteran presence I naturally enter upon this theme with diffidence; it is like an old maid trying to teach nursery matters to the mothers in Israel. It would not
10 become to me to criticize you, gentlemen—who are nearly all my elders—and my superiors, in this thing—if I should here and there *seem* to do it, I trust it will in most cases be more in a spirit of admiration than fault-finding; indeed if this finest of the fine arts had everywhere received the attention, the encouragement, and conscientious practice and development which this club has devoted to it, I should
15 not need to utter this lament, or shed a single tear. I do not say this to flatter: I say it in a spirit of just and appreciative recognition. [It had been my intention, at this point, to mention names and to give illustrative specimens, but indications observable about me admonished me to beware of the particulars and confine myself to generalities.]
20   No fact is more firmly established than that lying is a necessity of our circumstances—the deduction that it is then a Virtue goes without saying. No virtue can reach its highest usefulness without careful and diligent cultivation—therefore, it goes without saying that this one ought to be taught in the public schools—even in the newspapers. What chance has the ignorant uncultivated liar against the
25 educated expert? What chance have I against Mr. Per—against a lawyer? *Judicious* lying is what the world needs. I sometimes think it were even better and safer not to lie at all than to lie injudiciously. An awkward, unscientific lie is often as ineffectual as the truth.
    Now let us see what the philosophers say. Note that venerable proverb:
30 Children and fools *always* speak the truth. The deduction is plain—adults and wise persons *never* speak it. Parkman, the historian, says, "The principle of truth may itself be carried into an absurdity." In another place in the same chapters he says, "The saying is old that truth should not be spoken at all times; and those whom a sick conscience worries into habitual violation of the maxim are imbeciles and
35 nuisances." It is strong language, but true. None of us could *live* with an habitual

truth-teller; but thank goodness none of us has to. An habitual truth-teller is simply an impossible creature; he does not exist; he never has existed. Of course there are people who *think* they never lie, but it is not so—and this ignorance is one of the very things that shame our so-called civilization. Everybody lies—every day; every

40   hour; awake; asleep; in his dreams; in his joy; in his mourning; if he keeps his tongue still, his hands, his feet, his eyes, his attitude, will convey deception—and purposely. Even in sermons—but that is a platitude.

In a far country where I once lived the ladies used to go around paying calls, under the humane and kindly pretence of wanting to see each other; and when they

45   returned home, they would cry out with a glad voice, saying, "We made sixteen calls and found fourteen of them out"—not meaning that they found out anything important against the fourteen—no, that was only a colloquial phrase to signify that they were not at home—and their manner of saying it expressed their lively satisfaction in that fact. Now their pretence of wanting to see the fourteen—and the

50   other two whom they had been less lucky with—was that commonest and mildest form of lying which is sufficiently described as a deflection from the truth. Is it justifiable? Most certainly. It is beautiful, it is noble; for its object is, *not* to reap profit, but to convey a pleasure to the sixteen. The iron-souled truth monger would plainly manifest, or even utter the fact that he didn't want to see those people—and

55   he would be an ass, and inflict totally unnecessary pain. And next, those ladies in that far country—but never mind, they had a thousand pleasant ways of lying, that grew out of gentle impulses, and were a credit to their intelligence and an honor to their hearts. Let the particulars go.

The men in that far country were liars, every one. Their mere howdy-do was

60   a lie, because *they* didn't care how you did, except they were undertakers. To the ordinary inquirer you lied in return; for you made no conscientious diagnostic of your case, but answered at random, and usually missed it considerably. You lied to the undertaker, and said your health was failing—a wholly commendable lie, since it cost you nothing and pleased the other man. If a stranger called and interrupted

65   you, you said with your hearty tongue, "I'm glad to see you," and said with your heartier soul, "I wish you were with the cannibals and it was dinner-time." When he went, you said regretfully, "*Must* you go?" and followed it with a "Call again;" but you did no harm, for you did not deceive anybody nor inflict any hurt, whereas the truth would have made you both unhappy....

70   Joking aside, I think there is much need of wise examination into what sorts of lies are best and wholesomest to be indulged, seeing we *must* all lie and we *do* all lie, and what sorts it may be best to avoid—and this is a thing which I feel I can confidently put into the hands of this experienced Club—a ripe body, who may be termed, in this regard, and without undue flattery, Old Masters.

1. The purpose of the personification in lines 3-4 is to
    A. express the decline of lying.
    B. emphasize that the custom of lying is improving.
    C. suggest how lying is embedded in human nature.
    D. point out the inconveniences that lying can cause.

2. The "far country" mentioned in lines 43 and 59 most likely refers to
    F. Twain's contemporary society.
    G. Twain's visit to Italy in the 1850s.
    H. the way Twain feels society should be.
    J. the customs of the American West.

3. Based on the context, what is the most accurate meaning of the word
    diffidence (line 8)?
    A. diversity
    B. rigor
    C. arrogance
    D. timidity

4. The purpose of irony as used in lines 27-28 is to
    F. show the care that must be put into an effective lie.
    G. suggest that good lies are more useful than the truth.
    H. castigate people who lie poorly.
    J. express contempt for people who are too idealistic to lie.

5. What is the purpose of the lie told in lines paragraph 4 (lines 43-58)??
    A. to hide the ladies' fervent desire to see their friends
    B. to make their sixteen hosts feel better about themselves
    C. to demonstrate the "intelligence and honor" in their hearts
    D. to cover up a breach of etiquette

6. What might be the best alternative title for this passage?
    F. The Immorality of Deceit
    G. Where the Truth Lies
    H. Honesty is the Best Policy
    J. Truth and Lies in Other Countries

7. The overall tone of this passage is
    A. pedantic and scholarly.
    B. authoritative and impartial.
    C. sardonic and scornful.
    D. facetious and satiric.

8. What is the best way to paraphrase the sentence below (lines 31-32)?

    "The principle of truth may itself be carried into an absurdity."

    F. Being honest is ridiculous.
    G. Too much candor makes one ludicrous.
    H. People who follow principles are often persecuted with scorn.
    J. Carrying one's emotions around openly can lead to ridicule.

9. According to paragraph 3 (lines 29-42), what has come to be a "shame to our civilization"?
    A. the fact that people do not habitually tell the truth anymore
    B. the deceptive attitudes that characterize many people
    C. the fact that there are people who think they are always honest
    D. the idea that a truth-teller would be impossible to live with

10. This passage would most likely be found in
    F. a journal of American history.
    G. a doctoral dissertation.
    H. the opinion/editorial section of a newspaper.
    J. a handbook of literary criticism.

REVIEW
Lessons 8–14

Exercise I

Sentence Completion

Choose the best pair of words to complete the sentence. Most choices will fit grammatically and will even make sense logically, but you must choose the pair that best fits the idea of the sentence.

1. At his _____ laboratory disguised to look like a teddy bear factory, Dr. Insano worked feverishly on his _____ scheme to turn all the citizens of Maine into zombies.
   A. clandestine, heinous
   B. affable, unctuous
   C. feasible, inane
   D. omniscient, pernicious
   E. mundane, contrite

2. For her latest masterpiece, the artist used _____ found in the Arctic landscape that _____ feelings of desolation.
   A. effigies, impound
   B. hoaxes, emulate
   C. hues, evoke
   D. epistles, circumvent
   E. harangues, galvanize

3. The Internal Revenue Service _____ the actor who _____ the law for ten years in an attempt to avoid paying taxes.
   A. incarcerated, circumvented
   B. grimaced, cajoled
   C. abhorred, evinced
   D. acquitted, basked
   E. fluctuated, abated

4. Always _____ with her money, Lori _____ at buying the new car when the dealer tried to add several fees for processing the purchase.
    A. frugal, balked
    B. avid, chastised
    C. contrite, abated
    D. sere, exhorted
    E. latent, grimaced

5. If you don't want your romantic dinner to be a(n) _____, you should learn a few facts _____ to cooking seafood.
    A. decorum, implacable
    B. audacity, mundane
    C. fiasco, pertinent
    D. lethargy, dolorous
    E. sycophant, magnanimous

6. All of Harold's stories were filled with _____, so no one believed him when he claimed to have seen a(n) _____ bird trying to pluck a poodle off the ground.
    A. adulation, formidable
    B. hyperbole, gargantuan
    C. duplicity, pertinent
    D. effigy, fickle
    E. charlatan, ominous

7. The rising pop musician received so much _____ that she no longer possessed enough _____ to realize that her fans paid for her extravagant lifestyle.
    A. sanction, levity
    B. adulation, humility
    C. acrimony, duplicity
    D. grimace, juggernaut
    E. lethargy, métier

8. The _____ was accepted into evidence when the _____ claimed that the correspondence would exonerate his client.
    A. novice, evince
    B. epistle, barrister
    C. métier, dole
    D. myriad, abate
    E. hoax, expatriate

Exercise II

Crossword Puzzle

Use the clues to complete the crossword puzzle. The answers consist of vocabulary words from lessons 8 through 14.

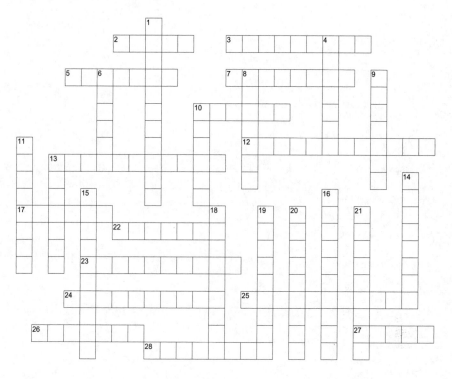

Across
2. to summon
3. relevant
5. friendly
7. sorrowful
10. likeness
12. stubborn
13. fight
17. strong point
22. to explain
23. insatiable
24. to bypass
25. unclear
26. difficult
27. to lessen
28. lecture

Down
1. to cooperate
4. to imitate
6. inconstant
8. threatening
9. propriety
10. to encourage
11. bitterness
13. strict
14. regretful
15. deadly
16. overjoyed
18. admiration
19. to spur into action
20. to deplore
21. a fraud

Book Two

Vocabulary
Power Plus
for the
ACT
Vocabulary,
Reading, and Writing
Exercises for High Scores

Lesson Fifteen

1. **noxious** (nok´shəs) *adj.* harmful to the health
   We opened a window to remove the *noxious* fumes of the paint thinner.
   syn: injurious   *ant: harmless*

2. **connive** (kə nīv´) *v.* to cooperate secretly in wrongdoing
   The corrupt judge *connived* with crooked politicians in order to make himself rich.
   syn: conspire

3. **chutzpah** (hoot´spə) *n.* nerve; audacity
   I cannot believe Michael had the *chutzpah* to claim that no one could sing that song as well as he could.
   syn: brazenness; effrontery   *ant: timidity*

4. **liege** (lēj) *n.* a lord, master, or sovereign
   While the servants pledged their loyalty to their *liege*, they did not always like or respect him.
   syn: king   *ant: commoner; servant*

5. **odium** (ō´dē əm) *n.* hatred
   The rebels had only *odium* for the ruling party.
   syn: abhorrence   *ant: love; adoration*

6. **crass** (kras) *adj.* coarse; tasteless
   Ben made a *crass* comment about the length of the waitress's skirt.
   syn: crude   *ant: refined*

7. **hypercritical** (hī pər krit´i kəl) *adj.* overcritical; too severe in judgment
   In his inspection of the barracks, the sergeant was so *hypercritical* that no one passed.
   syn: faultfinding   *ant: lax*

8. **fallacy** (fal´ə sē) *n.* a mistaken notion; a misconception
   My grandmother still clings to the *fallacy* that the world is flat.
   ant: truth

9. **complacent** (kəm plā′ sənt) *adj.* self-satisfied; smug
The former heavyweight champion became *complacent* after easily defeating several amateur boxers.
syn: assured; confident   *ant: humble*

10. **befuddle** (bi fud′ l) *v.* to confuse; to perplex
Street maps always *befuddle* me, so my girlfriend navigates when we take road trips.
syn: bewilder; fluster   *ant: clarify; elucidate*

11. **pandemonium** (pan də mō′ nē əm) *n.* a wild disorder, noise, or confusion
Feeding time at the zoo could be *pandemonium* if not done slowly and carefully.
syn: chaos; tumult; din   *ant: order; calm*

12. **parsimonious** (pär sə mō′ nē əs) *adj.* excessively thrifty; stingy
Ebenezer Scrooge was a *parsimonious* old man.
syn: cheap; frugal   *ant: extravagant*

13. **verbose** (vər bōs′) *adj.* using more words than are needed; wordy
Some find Charles Dickens so *verbose* that they swear he must have been paid by the word.
syn: prolix   *ant: terse; concise; succinct*

14. **laudable** (lô′ də bəl) *adj.* worthy of praise; commendable
The city has made *laudable* efforts to reduce crime by introducing after-school programs.
syn: admirable   *ant: execrable*

15. **indiscreet** (in di skrēt′) *adj.* not wise or judicious; imprudent, as in speech or action
Ron was fired shortly after his *indiscreet* actions at the office party.
syn: flagrant   *ant: prudent*

Exercise I

Words in Context

From the list below, supply the words needed to complete the paragraph. Some words will not be used.

odium	laudable	connived	verbose	befuddle
fallacy	noxious	chutzpah	crass	pandemonium

A.   If the company representative had arrived a minute later, the crowd would have erupted into _____. Since discovering the hidden toxic dump behind a residential neighborhood, most of the residents felt nothing but _____ for Kraytron officials. The whole mess began just two weeks before, when children became ill from inhaling _____ vapors in the forest next to their development. Two days, one evacuation, and one hazardous material response team later, town officials declared the site to be an illegal dump for hazardous waste. Though a thorough investigation would take months, if not years, most of the town's residents immediately concluded that Kraytron officials must have _____ with a few greedy local officials in an effort to avoid the cost of waste disposal.

When the booing and taunting finally stopped, the _____ Greg Haxton began his ninety-minute speech. Unknown to the public, Haxton had been Kraytron's unofficial crowd control specialist for over ten years.

"Your concern for your environment is indeed _____," said Greg. "It's good to see a community that can pull together in a predicament." Greg continued with his positive observations for five minutes before coming to the reason for his speech. "I know that many of you are assuming that Kraytron created the dump because the factory is only two miles from the site. This rumor is a complete _____; the officials have already dated the site as being at least twenty years old—ten years before Kraytron even constructed the local facility. The dump can be attributed to the _____ decisions of the former Mattingdon Aluminum Mill officials; they ran the mill here for forty years before going bankrupt two decades ago. To those of you who are Kraytron employees, you must understand that Kraytron would never have the _____ to commit such a heinous crime against its own family."

From the list below, supply the words needed to complete the paragraph. Some words will not be used.

befuddle	**liege**	**parsimonious**
chutzpah	**complacent**	**hypercritical**

B. "Come on, Jennifer, just buy a bag of charcoal! What are you going to save? Maybe a dime? I have never met a teenager as _____ as you."

   Silently mocking Julie, Jennifer grabbed the first bag of charcoal on the shelf. She knew that they were late for the cookout, but Julie's _____ attitude sometimes annoyed her. To Jennifer, it seemed as though Julie was always finding fault. They checked out at the register and walked to the car.

   "I'm sorry if this _____ you," remarked Jennifer, "but as it stands, we're broke, which means that we need to watch our spending. You've blown way too much money lately."

   Julie didn't reply immediately; she just sat in the patchwork seat of the primer-colored subcompact with a[n] _____ look on her face. As Jennifer turned the key, she heard Julie mumble a facetious "Yes, my _____."

Exercise II

Sentence Completion

Complete the sentence in a way that shows you understand the meaning of the italicized vocabulary word.

1. *Pandemonium* ensued at the stadium when...

2. Though she was a millionaire, the *parsimonious* woman still...

3. Your *verbose* lecture is causing the audience to...

4. The *liege* had only minutes to live, for the assassins were...

5. While working around *noxious* paint fumes, be sure to...

6. The emergency planning committee has made a *laudable* effort to protect the city from...

7. Leonard's *crass* demeanor sometimes caused Elmira to...

8. The *complacent* security guard had no idea that...

9. Though the apartment was immaculate, Lee's *hypercritical* mother still found...

10. The crooked commissioner *connived* with the mobster to...

11. Tawnya had the *chutzpah* to tell the speaker that...

12. Your *odium* for authority is only going to...

13. The *indiscreet* agent revealed his identity during...

14. Many people are guilty of believing the *fallacy* that...

15. Complicated math problems always *befuddled* Gene, which is why he...

Exercise III

Roots, Prefixes, and Suffixes

Study the entries and answer the questions that follow.

The roots *loqu* and *locut* mean "speak, talk."
The roots *pend* and *pens* mean "hang."
The root *gest* means "carry" or "bring."
The suffix *cy* means "the state or position of."
The prefix *e* means "out."

A. Using literal translations as guidance, define the following words without using a dictionary:

1. elocution
2. loquacious
3. eloquent
4. pendant
5. dependency
6. gestation

B. The crowd eagerly awaited the _____ outcome of the horse race while the judges analyzed the photo finish.

C. A *gesture* is a motion of the body that is used to express or emphasize ideas or emotions. Gesture comes from the root *gest*, but how is the word related to this root?

D. List as many words as you can think of that contain the roots *loqu*, *locut*, and *gest*.

Exercise IV

Inference

Complete the sentences by inferring information about the italicized word from its context.

A. If I am *hypercritical* while reviewing your work, and then you find a mistake in my work, you might tell me...

B. When the assembly instructions for a new appliance *befuddle* you, it is a good idea to...

C. When your boss reads your *indiscreet* remarks about the company in tomorrow's paper, she will probably...

Exercise V

Writing

Here is a writing prompt similar to the one you will find on the essay writing portion of the ACT.

> The traditional design of a school classroom has been the subject of jokes for decades, especially in the context of aging schools built with salmon-pink hallways leading to pale, drab classrooms. Critics claim that such schools are counterproductive to learning anything—that the color schemes and prison-like atmosphere practically declare failure. Architects traditionally design schools to ensure the efficient flow of people, but are schools ever built to help students think?
>
> Imagine you are an architect who has the opportunity to design a new high school for a district that has a total of 800 students (200 per graduating class). Choose a few key characteristics of your school and explain why the designs would be beneficial to students, and more conducive to learning than your present, real school setting. For your recommendation, consider the places where you personally read, write, study, and communicate most effectively.

Thesis: Write a *one-sentence* response to the above assignment. Make certain this single sentence offers a clear statement of your position.

Example: Schools should be designed to emulate environments in which the present generation truly feels interested and curious, such as among ancient ruins or scenic vistas.

_____

_____

Organizational Plan: List at least three subtopics you will use to support your main idea. This list is your outline.

1. _____

2. _____

3. _____

Draft: Following your outline, write a good first draft of your essay. Remember to support all your points with examples, facts, references to reading, etc.

Review and Revise: Exchange essays with a classmate. Using the scoring guide for Sentence Formation and Variety on page 227, score your partner's essay (while he or she scores yours). Focus on the sentence structure and use of language conventions. If necessary, rewrite your essay to improve the sentence structure and the use of language.

Exercise VI

English Practice

Improving Paragraphs

Read the following passage and then choose the best revision for the underlined portions of the paragraph. The questions will require you to make decisions regarding the revision of the reading selection. Some revisions are not of actual mistakes, but will improve the clarity of the writing.

[1]

Those of you who <u>are intimidated</u>[1] by the prospect of analyzing fiction need not worry any longer. Analyzing fiction is like analyzing anything else. Everything you see in front of you is a text: your book, your desk, the pencil in your hand, the outdated schedule on the wall—even the room you're sitting in. There is a trick, be warned: To analyze something, you need to pay attention at the details. If you look at a <u>pencil, for example, and say, "A pencil,"</u>[2] then you're not going to accomplish much; however, if you look at a pencil and take note of the unevenly worn lead, the bite marks obscuring the "Number 2" marking, and the tiny dent in the metal band retaining the dirty <u>eraser; then you're</u>[3] starting to analyze.

1. A. NO CHANGE
   B. is intimidated
   C. are intimidate
   D. is intimidation

2. F. NO CHANGE
   G. pencil for example and say,
      "A pencil,"
   H. pencil, for example, and
      say, A Pencil"
   J. pencil, for example, and
      say, "A pencil,"

3. A. NO CHANGE
   B. eraser, then you're
   C. eraser, then your
   D. eraser, then he or she is

[2]

(1)Once you note a few details that stand out, you can focus on one specific detail and apply some analytical questions to it: Why <u>is the lead worn unevenly.</u>[4] (2)Who uses this pencil? (3)What does this wear pattern tell me about the pencil? (4)<u>And yes, this</u>[5] might feel like detective work, but that is how proper analysis of a text should feel, because what is a crime scene but another text to analyze? (5)You might also ask yourself what color the pencil is because most people assume that pencils are yellow, but there are obviously many more colors.

4. F. NO CHANGE
   G. is the lead worn.
   H. is the lead worn unevenly?
   J. is the lead worn unevenly;

5. A. NO CHANGE
   B. But yes, this
   C. No doubt this
   D. However,

[3]

The more time you spend on the details, the greater the chance becomes that you will find connections between two details. When you reach this point, you have yet another <u>Focal Point</u>[6] that can be used for analysis and discussion. <u>Better yet. You might</u>[7] find that the details somehow contradict each other. Contradictions <u>literally beg you</u>[8] for your thoughts—your theories as to why a detail or an element of a text is, indeed, a contradiction.

6. F. NO CHANGE
   G. Focal point
   H. focal Point
   J. focal point

8. F. NO CHANGE
   G. practically beg you
   H. literally implore you
   J. especially try you

7. A. NO CHANGE
   B. Better yet—You might
   C. Better yet, you might
   D. You, better yet, might

[4]

Contradictions, details that don't seem to belong in the text, <u>and boring details that are so mundane that they seem entirely pointless,</u>[9] are analytical gold. While analyzing a text, assume nothing is accidental—otherwise the author (painter, sculptor, creator, etc.), would not have bothered including it. If your text is a short story or a poem, then each and every word you read is there intentionally and has meaning. <u>Why is the dried out earthworm mentioned by the author on the sidewalk?</u>[10] Why does the protagonist wear a particular brand of shoes? These details are not there just to take up space—they have meaning. A detail might have meaning that is relevant to only one element of the text, but you will not know <u>this until it's analyzed.</u>[11]

9. A. NO CHANGE
   B. and mundane details that seem entirely pointless
   C. and boring, mundane details that seem pointless
   D. and details, boring and mundane, that seem entirely pointless

10. F. NO CHANGE
    G. Why is the dried-out earthworm on the sidewalk mentioned by the author?
    H. Why does the author mention the dried-out earthworm on the sidewalk?
    J. Why is the earthworm, dried out and on the sidewalk, mentioned by the author?

11. A. NO CHANGE
    B. the relevance until that specific detail is analyzed.
    C. it until it's analyzed.
    D. its relevance until the detail is analyzed.

[5]

There <u>are people who believe it or not spend</u>[12] weeks, months, or years of their lives researching the tiniest details in texts. These people are known as scholars, and they command the secret that befuddles so many students who can't seem to find a good topic for their term papers—that the smaller the topic is, the better. Find that footnote, or that one awkward word that doesn't seem to belong with the others. <u>There's the beginning of your topic.</u>[13] You can spend minutes or hours explaining what that single item means to the whole text. That one little word or phrase or object is a portal to a whole realm of study. The value of the prize, of course, depends on the student, but the ultimate prize is the insight that the research yields.

12. F. NO CHANGE
    G. are people who believe it or not spend
    H. are people who believe it, or not, spend
    J. are people who, believe it or not, spend

13. A. NO CHANGE
    B. There is the beginning of your topic.
    C. There's the beginning of your topic directly in front of you.
    D. There's the beginning of your topic:

14. Which sentence would be the most appropriate final sentence for the passage?
    F. If the student can assign a value to the dried-out earthworm, then he or she has a prize.
    G. The research done, if it provides insight into the earthworm, is well worth it and possibly entertaining, too.
    H. If the research yields even a single original insight into the text, then the effort is worth it, and perhaps even interesting.
    J. So don't let literary analysis intimidate you; the more you simplify it, the more interesting it is.

15. If you had to delete an unnecessary or distracting sentence in paragraph 2, which one should it be?
    A. Sentence 2
    B. Sentence 3
    C. Sentence 4
    D. Sentence 5

Vocabulary
Power Plus
for the **ACT**
Vocabulary,
Reading, and Writing
Exercises for High Scores

Lesson Sixteen

1. **pique** (pēk) *v.* to cause resentment; to provoke
   The old gentleman was *piqued* because he was not given a seat at the head table.
   syn: irritate   *ant: assuage*

2. **linguistics** (ling gwis´ tiks) *n.* the scientific study of the structure, sounds, and meaning of language
   The professor of *linguistics* explained how English evolved from a number of other languages.

3. **plebeian** (pli bē´ ən) *n.* a commoner; one from the lower class
                             adj. common or vulgar
   (n.) Seniors treated the freshmen as though they were *plebeians*.
   (adj.) The baroness refused to do the *plebian* chores of cooking and cleaning.
   (n.) *syn: peon; peasant*   *ant: liege*
   (adj.) *syn: base; lowly*   *ant: refined; aristocratic*

4. **precocious** (pri kō´ shəs) *adj.* showing early development, especially mental
   Anthony was such a *precocious* three-year-old that he could already play the violin well.
   syn: advanced

5. **predatory** (pred´ ə tôr ē) *adj.* inclined to prey on others
   The buzzard is a scavenger, but the hawk is a *predatory* animal.
   syn: pillaging; despoiling   *ant: nurturing*

6. **prowess** (prow´ is) *n.* superior skill or ability
   Ty's physical *prowess* was matched by his superior mental ability.
   syn: strength; dominance; power   *ant: weakness*

7. **pugnacious** (pug nā´ shəs) *adj.* eager and ready to fight; quarrelsome
   Because he was so *pugnacious*, he had few friends.
   syn: combative; belligerent   *ant: placid; pacific*

8. **purloin** (pər loin´) *v.* to steal
   They had not planned to *purloin* the jewels, but the temptation was too great.
   syn: burglarize

9. **pusillanimous** (pyōō sə lan′ ə məs) *adj.* cowardly; fearful
The Wizard of Oz granted the *pusillanimous* lion his wish to have courage.
syn: fainthearted; timid   *ant: brave; bold*

10. **quell** (kwel) *v.* to put an end to; to allay or quiet
The police were called in to *quell* the riot.
syn: calm   *ant: foment; incite*

11. **quixotic** (kwik sot′ ik) *adj.* very idealistic; impractical; caught up in romantic notions
As a young man, he had the *quixotic* notion that he could single-handedly end poverty in the country.
                              ant: realistic; practical

12. **rabble** (rab′ əl) *n.* a disorderly crowd, a mob
The guards had to protect the president from the *rabble* in the streets.
syn: riffraff

13. **rabid** (rab′ id) *adj.* raging; fanatical
After working out, Chrissy had a *rabid* thirst and drank two gallons of water.
syn: uncontrollable; fervid   *ant: placid*

14. **raconteur** (rak on tyūr′) *n.* a person skilled at telling stories
An exceptional *raconteur*, Lorna held the whole audience spellbound with her stories.

15. **vindictive** (vin dik′ tiv) *adj.* seeking revenge; bearing a grudge
Out of some *vindictive* urge, Steve slashed his ex-girlfriend's tires.
syn: vengeful   *ant: forgiving*

Exercise I

Words in Context

From the list below, supply the words needed to complete the paragraph. Some words will not be used.

quell	**linguistics**	**vindictive**	**rabble**
prowess	**purloin**	**pugnacious**	

A. "Your _____ on the field does not excuse your _____ behavior at school. This is the second time that you've been in trouble for fighting," said the principal. She hated this situation; she knew what to do, but in the way the school perceived her, it would be a lose-lose decision. Punishing Isaac before the district championship game would surely draw a[n] _____ of angry students and parents to her office. Being lenient with Isaac would fuel the already _____ attitudes of second-offenders throughout the school. The turbulent aftermath of either decision would be difficult to _____.

From the list below, supply the words needed to complete the paragraph. Some words will not be used.

plebeian **pique** **raconteur** **quell** **linguistics** **precocious**

B. Everyone had high hopes for the _____ youngster. At the age of six, Mariah seemed to have such a command of _____ that a simple conversation with her might easily arouse anger and _____ in even the brightest of her classmates; consequently, they felt as though they were speaking to an adult, rather than to a child. She also loved to exercise her fine speaking abilities. Never at a loss for words, the young _____ would come home from school every night and vividly describe the events of her day to her parents.

From the list below, supply the words needed to complete the paragraph. Some words will not be used.

plebeian	quixotic	linguistics	pusillanimous
predatory	rabid	purloin	

C.   Owing in part to his _____ interest in the heroic tales of Arthur's knights set in the Middle Ages, Delmar had a rather _____ perspective of the world. He never simply "went to work" or "picked up a burger at the drive-through"; instead, Delmar lived in a fantasy world in which each day he had to uphold his chivalric duty while challenging a myriad of perilous obstacles. The pigeons on the roof of his apartment were not pigeons—they were great, _____ winged beasts, perpetually waiting to swoop down and _____ Delmar's poppyseed bagel as he walked to his chariot—a rusty Ford Granada that had recently passed the two-hundred-thousand-mile mark. After a short ride to the Hall of Lords (the metro station), Delmar would spend the day protecting the ignorant _____ from microscopic legions of evil warriors, mainly by spraying all surfaces with disinfectant before wiping them down with a rag. Evil dirt warriors were not Delmar's greatest problem; sometimes he had to confront the mystical rat-beasts that lived in the basement storage area. Indeed, the basement was no place for _____ folk—only knights as brave as Sir Delmar.

Exercise II

Sentence Completion

Complete the sentence in a way that shows you understand the meaning of the italicized vocabulary word.

1. Carnivorous *predatory* animals will eat meat before they will eat...

2. The filthy tavern was full of *pugnacious* characters looking for...

3. Let's see if your *prowess* during practice extends to the...

4. The *rabble* outside the governor's mansion chanted about the new policy on...

5. The tear gas easily *quelled* the protestors at...

6. The audience was engrossed with the old *raconteur's* accounts of…

7. Everyone knew that Colt was too *pusillanimous* to ever become a professional…

8. The *quixotic* Dexter thought that he alone could someday…

9. The new *linguistics* teacher claimed that writing was just as important as…

10. After three days of surviving in the wilderness, the co-pilot's *rabid* hunger drove her to…

11. The dressmaker *piqued* Linda by pointing out that she…

12. Still *vindictive* about losing the promotion to a younger associate, Elvira made life…

13. After he *purloined* the company secrets, Sol went to the competition and…

14. The *precocious* preschooler was already good at…

15. The greedy Duke never responded to the *plebeian* requests for…

Exercise III

Roots, Prefixes, and Suffixes

Study the entries and answer the questions that follow.

> The root *man* means "hand."
> The suffix *escent* means "becoming."
> The roots *nat* and *nas* mean "born."
> The prefix *in* means "in."
> The prefix *re* means "again."

A. *Using literal translations as guidance, define the following words without using a dictionary:*

1. manacles
2. innate
3. nativity
4. nascent
5. renascence
6. manicure

B. Literally, *manual labor* is labor _____.
    The word "manufacture" contains two roots: _____ and _____.
    It literally means _____.
    Manipulation literally refers to _____,
    and the word *manuscript* literally means _____.

C. A *mandate* is an order or a command. How do you think this word got its meaning?

D. List all the words you can think of that have the suffix *escent*.

E. List all the words that you can think of that contain the roots *nat* or *nas*.

Exercise IV

Inference

Complete the sentences by inferring information about the italicized word from its context.

A. Gwendolyn and the Duke of Trombonia loved each other, but since Gwendolyn was a *plebeian*, they...

B. Geoff is very *pugnacious*, so if someone accidentally spills a beverage on him, he will probably...

C. If the police are sent to *quell* a riot, they might...

Exercise V

Critical Reading

Below is a reading passage followed by several multiple-choice questions similar to the ones you will encounter on the ACT. Carefully read the passage and choose the best answer to each of the questions.

The author of this passage is commenting on the creation of empires.

A system of trade transpires when a nation's demand for goods obliges it to seek these products from other nations. England needed goods that it could not produce because of an improper climate or a lack of necessary resources; consequently, it sent explorers to find the materials in foreign lands. The exploration found not only
5   the required goods, but new, previously unknown lands and peoples with whom England could establish new commerce. The discovery of the new lands was an impetus for travel and colonization, which in turn resulted in new technology and economic advancement of the mother country.

Even in its early stages, a functional system of international trade required
10 considerable travel and enormous logistical effort. To ensure the success of established trade routes, merchants had to maintain a presence in other nations, especially those that were undeveloped and thus potential trade partners for other nations. These agents, or representatives, would establish trading posts in which they could acquire the native goods and transfer them to the traders or merchants.
15 As trade increased, more people were required to support acquisition efforts. In response to growing demand, England established colonies that were capable of conducting the necessary business while protecting goods, shipments, and relations with the host nations; however, relations were not always ideal for the natives. Many of the merchant colonists sought advancement in social status, and they favored the
20 idea that despite having a low social status at home, they were far superior to the often-primitive natives. On the grounds of their perceived superiority, colonists acquired goods, land, and labor at little cost. Mother countries sought to "civilize" the natives, which, to the colonists, meant compelling the natives to emulate the language, culture, and religion of the mother country.
25 Expansion of trade forced leaps in technology, beginning with advancements in transportation. The growing number of colonists and merchants required a means of transporting themselves and their goods. Larger and faster ships emerged, allowing more efficient international commerce. Traders could transfer more goods, make more frequent trips, and communicate more quickly with their counterparts
30 abroad. The invention of the telegraph accelerated commerce even more, because merchants could instantly exchange knowledge about demand, prices, or shipping details across great distances. Medical advancements also increased commerce; the discovery of quinine helped traders to overcome the deadly malaria that was rampant throughout certain colonies. By diminishing the threat of disease, traders
35 and colonists could remain in foreign lands for extended periods while pushing inland to expand trade opportunities.

After establishing an efficient system of international trade, the mother country was able to soar to economic superiority and get rid of its own abundance of goods, particularly those made using the raw materials imported from colonies. The
40 mother country manufactured products from the goods and exported them back to the colonized country—a process that was patently unfair to the colonized country but especially profitable for the mother country, which, consequently, increased in wealth. To protect these interests, the mother country maintained a military presence in the colonies while forcing the assimilation of the natives to its own
45 cultural and political systems. Eventually, smaller countries in the trade network would be forced to limit trade to only the mother country, thus making them economically dependent. They became small components of what is defined as an empire.

1. Choose the choice that best summarizes the flow of events that lead to the creation of an empire, as esponged in the passage.
    A. Colonization creates a demand for wealth, so the mother nation begins to explore new lands and discover new technology.
    B. New technology allows the establishment of trade routes, which ultimately yields new lands and larger economies.
    C. The search for resources yields new lands and colonization and the necessary new technology to support it.
    D. New lands are sought in order to create demand for new technology and rapid economic development.

2. The overall tone of this passage is
    F. entertaining.
    G. thoughtful.
    H. simplistic.
    J. scholarly.

3. According to paragraph two (lines 9-24), initial colonization resulted from the need to
    A. have trade representatives in the distant nations.
    B. help people advance in social status.
    C. find places to send missionaries.
    D. civilize the natives.

4. As used in line 8, *mother* means
    F. one who gives birth.
    G. a female parent.
    H. a woman of authority.
    J. the source or origin of something.

5. Which of the following best paraphrases the sentence, "Mother countries
    sought to 'civilize' the natives, which, to the colonists, meant compelling
    the natives to emulate the language, culture, and religion of the mother
    country" (line 22-24)?
    A. The British were the only civilized people.
    B. Colonists thought they were the only civilized people.
    C. All native cultures were uncivilized.
    D. Colonists felt superior to all people.

6. Which of the following is an example of how technology did *not* grow
    because of trade?
    F. the development of faster ships
    G. the discovery of quinine
    H. the invention of the telegraph
    J. the development of mass production

7. As used in line 33, *quinine* most likely means a type of
    A. beverage.
    B. precious metal.
    C. medicine.
    D. transportation.

8. According to paragraph four (lines 37-48), which is *not* a reason why trade
    is beneficial?
    F. disposal of extra goods
    G. attainment of wanted goods
    H. ability to manufacture products
    J. higher revenue for the mother country

9. Which choice would be the best title for this passage?
    A. Trade as a Dominant Force in Creating Empires
    B. How Empires are Created in History
    C. Trade, Travel, and Technology
    D. Empires and Their Economies

10. This passage would most likely be found in
    F. an encyclopedia of economics.
    G. a book of empires.
    H. a doctoral dissertation.
    J. a world history book.

Vocabulary
Power Plus
for the ACT

Vocabulary,
Reading, and Writing
Exercises for High Scores

Lesson Seventeen

1. **circumspect** (sûr´ kəm spekt) *adj.* careful; heedful; attentive to all
   points
   Although I tried to be *circumspect* about my friends, I never guessed that
   one of them had a criminal record.
   syn: judicious; prudent   *ant: rash; foolhardy*

2. **zephyr** (zef´ ər) *n.* a gentle breeze (sometimes specifically the West Wind)
   A sweet-smelling *zephyr* ruffled the laundry on the line.
                                                 ant: gale

3. **renegade** (ren´ i gād) *n.* one who deserts one side in favor of another;
   traitor; outlaw
   The members of the old party called him a *renegade*; the members of his
   new party called him a patriot.
   syn: turncoat; defector   *ant: loyalist*

4. **retribution** (ret rə byōō´ shən) *n.* something justly deserved,
   especially a punishment
   The boys had to spend the weekend picking up litter in *retribution* for
   having spray-painted graffiti on the bus.
   syn: reprisal   *ant: reward*

5. **hurtle** (hûr´ tl) *v.* to move or to fling swiftly and with great force
   The big fullback *hurtled* his way through the defensive line and scored the
   winning touchdown.
   syn: hurl

6. **scourge** (skûrj) *n.* a person or thing that causes great trouble or
   misfortune
   Cancer remains one of the worst *scourges* of mankind.
   syn: torment; bane; curse   *ant: boon; blessing*

7. **caustic** (kô´ stik) *adj.* biting; stingingly sharp or sarcastic; highly irritating
   Because of his *caustic* comments, his wife finally left him.
   syn: acidic; harsh   *ant: mild; pleasant*

8. **taciturn** (tas´ i tûrn) *adj.* not fond of talking; usually silent
   We were amazed when the *taciturn* young man signed up for public speaking.
   syn: *reticent; reserved*   ant: *garrulous; loquacious; talkative*

9. **agnostic** (ag nos´ tik) *n.* one who believes that the existence of God can neither be proved nor disproved
   Although he did not officially believe in God, the *agnostic* sometimes prayed "just in case."
   syn: *skeptic*   ant: *believer*

10. **terse** (tûrs) *adj.* brief and to the point
    Julia didn't give me any details about her break-up, just a *terse* "it's over."
    syn: *abbreviated; curt*   ant: *verbose; rambling*

11. **uncanny** (un kan´ ē) *adj.* weird; strange; so keen or acute as to seem bizarre
    Tess had an *uncanny* memory for details; she knew exactly what she had worn on any given day in the past eleven years.
    syn: *eerie*

12. **exodus** (ek´ sə dəs) *n.* a mass departure or emigration
    The many defeated tribes made a speedy *exodus* from the war-torn valley.
                                                        ant: *return*

13. **penitent** (pen´ i tənt) *adj.* remorseful; sorry for having done wrong
    Seeing the boy's *penitent* expression, the judge was easier on him than he might otherwise have been.
    syn: *apologetic*   ant: *unrepentant*

14. **vindicate** (vin´ di kāt) *v.* to clear of suspicion or accusations
    Darren sued for libel in order to *vindicate* his reputation.
    syn: *exonerate; acquit*   ant: *besmirch; implicate*

15. **raillery** (rā´ lə rē) *n.* good-humored ridicule or teasing
    James much prefers Carson's *raillery* to the cynical slurs of other comedians.
    syn: *banter*

Exercise I

Words in Context

From the list below, supply the words needed to complete the paragraph. Some words will not be used.

| penitent | hurtle | agnostic | scourge |
| circumspect | retribution | zephyr | exodus |

A. Sergeant Neil Newman, one of six mine removal experts in Southeast Asia, makes sure that he is _____ about every aspect of his job.
"One little missed detail can result in tragedy becoming a sort of _____ for your hastiness. One minute you're on your knees, probing the earth and enjoying a cool _____ after hours of 95-degree weather, and the next minute, a blast _____ you—or a part of you—through the air because you overlooked a hair-thin tripwire. By that time, it's too late to be _____ about your error—you're lucky if you're still alive to think about it."
The uncharted minefields that Neil faces have been a[n] _____ on war-torn nations for decades, and experts estimate that it will take people like Neil hundreds of years to find and neutralize the millions of underground threats.

From the list below, supply the words needed to complete the paragraph. Some words will not be used.

| raillery | vindicate | terse | taciturn |
| hurtle | uncanny | exodus | renegade |

B. The _____ Haley silently stared at her console despite the elated atmosphere of the command center. While everyone celebrated the latest victory of the rebel forces, Haley received a message that would soon turn the celebration into panic. Two _____ had revealed the secret location of the command center, and as soon as she gave the word, the entire facility would have to prepare for a[n] _____ to a new location before the Nationalist forces arrived. The Nationalists had a[n] _____ ability to turn the rebels against each other; this would be the third time in three months that the rebels were forced to relocate their base of operations. Haley took a breath, swiveled around in her chair, and prepared to deliver a[n] _____ briefing that would squelch the group's cheerful air. To make matters worse, one of the traitors turned out to be Haley's cousin, a lieutenant whom Haley recently helped _____ from espionage charges.

From the list below, supply the words needed to complete the paragraph. Some words will not be used.

terse   raillery   caustic   agnostic   scourge

C.   Paige and Mia have been friends for more than twenty years, despite the fact that Paige is devoutly religious and Mia is a[n] _____. They often have heated discussions about religion, but their conversation inevitably turns into good-humored _____. Over the years, they learned to avoid making _____ comments during an argument, no matter how angry they might get.

Exercise II

Sentence Completion

Complete the sentence in a way that shows you understand the meaning of the italicized vocabulary word.

1.   The workers were thankful for the *zephyr* as they labored through the...

2.   The victims of the bombing demanded *retribution* for their...

3.   The asteroid *hurtled* toward earth, giving the people only minutes to...

4.   Sheila's *caustic* tongue made her supervisor think twice about...

5.   Major Buchanan gave a *terse* briefing about the invading squadron of...

6.   The acrobatic trio had the *uncanny* ability to...

7.   Urik's family finally *vindicated* him after he spent eight years in prison for...

8.   Though his parents were bothered by it, Thomas remained an *agnostic* in...

9.   The *renegade* mercenary quietly left his platoon in order to...

10.   The *circumspect* fashion designer made sure the dress...

11.   Good humored *raillery* did not please the new teacher, who in turn...

12. The maniacal dictator was a *scourge* on mankind until…

13. The *taciturn* Willow surprised everyone when she decided to become…

14. The penitent *fugitive* decided to stop running and…

15. As the last stone was removed from the cave entrance, an *exodus* of…

Exercise III

Roots, Prefixes, and Suffixes

Study the entries and answer the questions that follow.

The root *phil* means "love" or "loving."
The root *ocul* means "eye."
The root *mar* means "sea."
The prefix *sub* means "under."

A. *Using literal translations as guidance, define the following words without using a dictionary:*

    1. philanthropy   4. ocular
    2. philharmonic   5. oculist
    3. maritime   6. submarine

B. The root *sophos* means wise, so a *philosopher* is one who _____
    _____.
    The root *moros* means "foolish" or "fool"; therefore, the literal meaning of "sophomore" is _____.

C. *Phile* is sometimes found at the end of a word. What do you suppose the following people love?
    anglophiles:
    francophiles:
    bibliophiles:

D. List all the words you can think of that contain the roots *phil*, *ocul* or *mar*.

Exercise IV

Inference

Complete the sentences by inferring information about the italicized word from its context.

A. If Mr. Reckner cannot *vindicate* himself from the charges of grand larceny, he will probably…

B. Damian, who went to school despite the fact that he was sick with influenza, became the *scourge* of his class when…

C. The pianist didn't even need an electronic tuner; she had the *uncanny* ability to…

Exercise V

Writing

Here is a writing prompt similar to the one you will find on the essay writing portion of the ACT.

Plan and write an essay based on the following statement:

> The subject of wages and salary might seem like a distant concern for students who have yet to commit to a job or career, but it is all too real for people in the working world, who must prove their own value on a daily basis by producing a product or providing a service. Unsurprisingly, there is as much disparity among wage earners as there is among personality types of everyone on Earth.
>
> Consider one career choice that is known to pay a large salary both and one career in which the wages are far too low. Argue whether the careers you select should or should not command high wages, comparing them in the process.
>
> Support your arguments with facts, details, and examples, and remember to address counterarguments to your position while you construct your essay.

Thesis: Write a *one-sentence* response to the above assignment. Make certain this single sentence offers a clear statement of your position.

Example: It is embarrassing that the people who are required to be in harm's way on a daily basis earn a fraction of those people who simply entertain bored people for a living.

_____

_____

Organizational Plan: List at least three subtopics you will use to support your main idea. This list is your outline.

1. _____

2. _____

3. _____

Draft: Following your outline, write a good first draft of your essay. Remember to support all your points with examples, facts, references to reading, etc.

Review and Revise: Exchange essays with a classmate. Using the scoring guide for Word Choice on page 228, score your partner's essay (while he or she scores yours). Focus on word choice and the use of language conventions. If necessary, rewrite your essay to improve the word choice and the use of language.

Exercise VI

English Practice

Identifying Sentence Errors
Identify the errors in the following sentences. Choose the answer that fixes the error. If the sentence contains no error, select answer NO CHANGE.

1. When the warden agreed with us that the prisoner <u>should be released; we were pleased</u> to accept the invitation to the parole hearing.
   A. NO CHANGE
   B. should be released: we were pleased
   C. should be released we were pleased
   D. should be released, we were pleased

2. The new park project for underprivileged children <u>began</u> in the spring, but will not be completed until late November.
   F. NO CHANGE
   G. was began
   H. had began
   J. begun

3. Last year, we had an especially severe winter and despite our efforts to remove the snow, it <u>had lain</u> on the barn roof all season.
   A. NO CHANGE
   B. had laid
   C. had layed
   D. lay

4. When all the votes are in and are counted, <u>it alone</u> will decide the next governor of this fine state.
    F. NO CHANGE
    G. they alone
    H. it
    J. they alone it

5. The speaker at the horse-breeders' convention would have been better if <u>she took the time</u> to prepare for the subjects of interest to the audience.
    A. NO CHANGE
    B. had took the time
    C. had taken the time
    D. would have took the time

Improving Sentences

The underlined portion of each sentence below contains some flaw. Select the answer that best corrects the flaw.

6. The aging movie star was particular about her appearance, but <u>was as particularly engaging as ever</u> when she looked her best.
    F. was as particular as engaging as ever
    G. was as engaging particularly as ever
    H. was as engaging as ever
    J. was particularly engaging

7. <u>We were bouncing a basketball and a neighbor came over then and told us we were making too much noise being in the driveway.</u>
    A. We were bouncing a basketball in the driveway, and a neighbor came over to tell us we were making too much noise.
    B. A neighbor came over to tell us we were making too much noise and we were bouncing a basketball in the driveway.
    C. We were bouncing a basketball because a neighbor in the driveway came over to tell us we were making too much noise.
    D. Bouncing a basketball, a neighbor came over and told us we were making too much noise in the driveway.

8. Hoping for the support of his constituents the incumbent candidate who ran against a strong opponent for the position of state senator.
   F. Hoping his constituents would support him, the incumbent candidate for state senator faced a strong opponent.
   G. Running against a strong opponent was an incumbent state senator candidate who hoped for constituent support.
   H. Hoping to be state senator, the incumbent candidate ran against a strong opponent, and he was hoping for the support of his constituents.
   J. The incumbent candidate, a state senator, was hoping for the support of his constituents while running against a strong opponent for his seat.

9. Alfred was able to secure a government job after he graduated from college which lasted for almost twenty years.
   A. Alfred lasted almost twenty years after he was able to secure a government job after he graduated from college.
   B. Alfred was able to graduate from college to secure a government job which lasted for almost twenty years.
   C. After graduating from college, Alfred was able to secure a government job that lasted for almost twenty years.
   D. For almost twenty years, Alfred was able to secure a government job after he graduated from college.

10. When children play in the street without any shoes and their mothers know about it and the neighbors don't tell them to stop.
    F. Neighbors shouldn't tell their children to stop when they play in the street without shoes and their mothers know about it.
    G. When children play in the street without any shoes, and their mothers know about it, the neighbors won't stop them from playing.
    H. When neighbors don't tell them to stop, children play in the street without any shoes and their mothers know about it.
    J. Without shoes, children play in the street and their mothers know about it and the neighbors don't tell them to stop.

Book Two

Vocabulary
Power Plus
for the
ACT
Vocabulary,
Reading, and Writing
Exercises for High Scores

Lesson Eighteen

1. **impregnable**   (im preg´ nə bəl)   *adj.*   not able to be conquered; impenetrable
The Greek warriors were unable to conquer the *impregnable* Trojan fortress.
syn: unbeatable   *ant: vulnerable*

2. **xenophobia**   (ze nə fō´ bē ə)   *n.*   an intense dislike or fear of strangers or foreigners
Tim's *xenophobia* gave him an unwarranted hatred for immigrants coming to America.

3. **inherent**   (in hir´ ənt)   *adj.*   essential
Emissions causing air pollution is the major *inherent* drawback of the automobile.
syn: intrinsic   *ant: extrinsic; extraneous*

4. **irreverent**   (i rev´ rənt)   *adj.*   disrespectful
John's *irreverent* attitude toward his pastor embarrassed and angered his mother.
syn: insubordinate   *ant: worshipful*

5. **subjugate**   (sub´ ji gāt)   *v.*   to dominate, conquer, or bring under control
The invaders *subjugated* the natives and forced them to do manual labor.
syn: repress   *ant: free*

6. **expedite**   (ek´ spə dīt)   *v.*   to increase the rate of progress
More construction workers were brought on to the project to help *expedite* the construction of the new bridge.
syn: hurry; hasten; streamline   *ant: retard; hinder*

7. **filibuster**   (fil´ ə bəs tər)   *v.*   to attempt to block a bill from becoming law by speaking at length against it
The Senator from Mississippi gave an eight-hour speech to *filibuster* the new tax bill.
syn: derail

8. **pristine** (pris´ tēn) *adj.* pure; completely clean and uncontaminated
The vast, *pristine* wilderness of northern Alaska is too cold and remote for most people to inhabit.
syn: pure   *ant: defiled; spoiled; sullied*

9. **pithy** (pi´ thē) *adj.* full of meaning; concise
The *pithy* statements in greeting cards are often short and sweet.
syn: succinct   *ant: verbose*

10. **invective** (in vek´ tiv) *n.* an insult or abuse in speech
Scott's *invective*, aimed at his teacher, resulted in an immediate trip to the principal's office.
syn: reproach   *ant: praise*

11. **prodigal** (prä´ di gəl) *adj.* reckless, wasteful, and extravagant
The *prodigal* actor was notorious for his lavish, excessive, and unruly lifestyle.
syn: wastrel; libertine   *ant: prudent*

12. **pliable** (plī´ ə bəl) *adj.* easily bent or flexible
NASA had to devise a new, more *pliable* spacesuit for astronauts working on the the space station.
                                             ant: rigid

13. **torpid** (tōr´ ped) *adj.* losing motion, feeling, or power; lacking in energy
The sleeping gas caused the hero's mind to become *torpid*.
syn: apathetic; lethargic   *ant: energetic*

14. **tenuous** (ten´ yə wəs) *adj.* not dense or thick; having little substance
Even though it was published, the dissertation put forth a very *tenuous* theory on animal intelligence.
syn: thin; unconvincing; fragile   *ant: strong; cogent*

15. **discordant** (dis kōrd´ dənt) *adj.* being in disagreement
The angry and *discordant* voices echoed throughout the conference room.
syn: conflicting   *ant: harmonious*

Exercise I

Words in Context

From the list below, supply the words needed to complete the paragraph. Some words will not be used.

pristine	discordant	xenophobia	subjugate
impregnable	invective	pithy	inherent

A.   Queen Alana's _____ was not entirely unfounded. During her twenty-year reign, her lands had been the victim of four separate invasions, two of which nearly _____ the tiny island to foreign rule. The enemies had already expressed views that were _____ with the Queen's about common borders. After issuing a fiery _____ questioning the foreign king's intentions, Queen Alana began to prepare for war. Two days later, the _____, old-world forest on the southern shore of her realm became crowded with invading troops, all of whom were preparing for an onslaught on the supposedly _____ castle.

From the list below, supply the words needed to complete the paragraph. Some words will not be used.

irreverent	filibuster	prodigal	torpid
inherent	expedite	pithy	tenuous

B.   Despite four thousand years of erosion, the Egyptian hieroglyphics on the wall still carried a[n] _____ message: "Enter and be doomed." Murdoch, trying to _____ stealing the hidden treasure, paid no attention to the symbols as he raised his pickaxe over his head and sent it crashing into, but not through, the limestone wall. The native guide scolded Murdoch's _____ treatment of the ancient burial chamber, but Murdoch retorted with the quick explanation that etiquette was not a[n] _____ part of archaeological theft. Murdoch took a _____, second swing, this time penetrating the wall. He grinned at the thought of what waited for him beyond the wall, unaware that the guide had become pale and stood in amazement next to the catacomb entrance, _____ and unable to escape.

From the list below, supply the words needed to complete the paragraph. Some words will not be used.

filibuster	prodigal	pliable
xenophobia	torpid	invective

C.   Senator Melita Darnell knew that she would have to _____ to prevent a vote on the new McDermid Bill. To her, the bill would pave the way for the same _____ government spending that she had vowed to eliminate; unfortunately, the opinions of the committee were fixed, and not _____ enough for her to sway anyone prior to the session. She was going to have to do this the hard way.

Exercise II

Sentence Completion

Complete the sentence in a way that shows you understand the meaning of the italicized vocabulary word.

1.   The car collector could tell by the *pristine* condition of the coupe that...

2.   The *prodigal* lifestyle of the twin sisters caused the family to...

3.   Many of the laborers became *torpid* when the weather...

4.   The surgeon called from Nebraska to tell the Maryland courier to *expedite* the...

5.   The advertising department sought a *pithy* catchphrase for...

6.   *Discordant* union members were blamed for lost work during the...

7.   Owing to unfounded *xenophobia*, some citizens fear...

8.   Ancient Rome *subjugated* its captured prisoners by...

9.   The *impregnable* underground base proved to be impossible to...

10. *Pliable* eyeglass frames prevent the wearer from accidentally...

11. An *inherent* part of college life is...

12. The *tenuous* criticism of the show did not...

13. The representative's *filibuster* prevented Congress from...

14. Irene's loud *invective* to Jye caused everyone within earshot to...

15. The mourners thought that Niles was *irreverent* to talk on his cell phone during...

Exercise III

Roots, Prefixes, and Suffixes

Study the entries and answer the questions that follow.

The roots *luc, lus, and lum* mean "light."
The prefix *il* means "in."
The root *ten* means "to hold."
The roots *cur* and *cours* mean "to run" or "to go."

A. Using literal translations as guidance, define the following words without using a dictionary:

   1. illuminate   4. current
   2. curriculum   5. tenant
   3. tenet   6. luminosity

B. The root *lieu* means "place," so the literal translation of *lieutenant* is
   _____.
   If you deliver packages for people by running them from one place to another, your job title might be _____.

C. If *trans* means "through," then *translucent* means _____.
   If you prefer a particular brand of bread, then you probably have a[n]
   _____ to purchase that brand when you go shopping.

D. List all the words you can think of that contain the roots *lus, luc,* or *ten.*

E. List all the words you can think of that contain the roots *cur* or *cours.*

Exercise IV

Inference

Complete the sentences by inferring information about the italicized word from its context.

A. The security company told Iniko that his house was *impregnable*, so he was surprised when he got home and discovered that...

B. Someone going to a country in which the climate is *torpid* should...

C. When you hear one driver shout *invectives* at another driver, you might assume that...

Exercise V

Critical Reading

Below is a reading passage followed by several multiple-choice questions similar to the ones you will encounter on the ACT. Carefully read the passage and choose the best answer to each of the questions.

The following passage is adapted from Chapter 113, "The Forge," from Herman Melville's <u>Moby Dick</u>.

With matted beard, and swathed in a bristling shark-skin apron, about mid-day, Perth was standing between his forge and anvil, the latter placed upon an iron-wood log, with one hand holding a pike-head in the coals, and with the other at his forge's lungs, when Captain Ahab came along, carrying in his hand a small rusty-looking
5   leathern bag. While yet a little distance from the forge, moody Ahab paused; till at last, Perth, withdrawing his iron from the fire, began hammering it upon the anvil—the red mass sending off the sparks in thick hovering flights, some of which flew close to Ahab.

"Are these thy Mother Carey's chickens, Perth? they are always flying in thy
10   wake; birds of good omen, too, but not to all;—look here, they burn; but thou—thou liv'st among them without a scorch."

"Because I am scorched all over, Captain Ahab," answered Perth, resting for a moment on his hammer; "I am past scorching; not easily can'st thou scorch a scar."

"Well, well; no more. Thy shrunk voice sounds too calmly, sanely woeful to me.
15   In no Paradise myself, I am impatient of all misery in others that is not mad. Thou should'st go mad, blacksmith; say, why dost thou not go mad? How can'st thou endure without being mad? Do the heavens yet hate thee, that thou can'st not go mad?—What wert thou making there?"

"Welding an old pike-head, sir; there were seams and dents in it."
20   "And can'st thou make it all smooth again, blacksmith, after such hard usage as it had?"

"I think so, sir."

"And I suppose thou can'st smoothe almost any seams and dents; never mind how hard the metal, blacksmith?"
25   "Aye, sir, I think I can; all seams and dents but one."

"Look ye here, then," cried Ahab, passionately advancing, and leaning with both hands on Perth's shoulders; "look ye here—HERE—can ye smoothe out a seam like this, blacksmith," sweeping one hand across his ribbed brow; "if thou could'st, blacksmith, glad enough would I lay my head upon thy anvil, and feel thy heaviest
30   hammer between my eyes. Answer! Can'st thou smoothe this seam?"

"Oh! that is the one, sir! Said I not all seams and dents but one?"

"Aye, blacksmith, it is the one; aye, man, it is unsmoothable; for though thou only see'st it here in my flesh, it has worked down into the bone of my skull—THAT is all wrinkles! But, away with child's play; no more gaffs and pikes to-day. Look
35   ye here!" jingling the leathern bag, as if it were full of gold coins. "I, too, want a harpoon made; one that a thousand yoke of fiends could not part, Perth; something

that will stick in a whale like his own fin-bone. There's the stuff," flinging the pouch upon the anvil. "Look ye, blacksmith, these are the gathered nail-stubs of the steel shoes of racing horses."

40   "Horse-shoe stubbs, sir? Why, Captain Ahab, thou hast here, then, the best and stubbornest stuff we blacksmiths ever work."

"I know it, old man; these stubbs will weld together like glue from the melted bones of murderers. Quick! forge me the harpoon. And forge me first, twelve rods for its shank; then wind, and twist, and hammer these twelve together like the yarns 45 and strands of a tow-line. Quick! I'll blow the fire."

When at last the twelve rods were made, Ahab tried them, one by one, by spiralling them, with his own hand, round a long, heavy iron bolt. "A flaw!" rejecting the last one. "Work that over again, Perth."

This done, Perth was about to begin welding the twelve into one, when Ahab 50 stayed his hand, and said he would weld his own iron. As, then, with regular, gasping hems, he hammered on the anvil, Perth passing to him the glowing rods, one after the other, and the hard pressed forge shooting up its intense straight flame, the Parsee passed silently, and bowing over his head towards the fire, seemed invoking some curse or some blessing on the toil. But, as Ahab looked up, he slid 55 aside.

"What's that bunch of lucifers dodging about there for?" muttered Stubb, looking on from the forecastle. "That Parsee smells fire like a fusee; and smells of it himself, like a hot musket's powder-pan."

At last the shank, in one complete rod, received its final heat; and as Perth, to 60 temper it, plunged it all hissing into the cask of water near by, the scalding steam shot up into Ahab's bent face.

"Would'st thou brand me, Perth?" wincing for a moment with the pain; "have I been but forging my own branding-iron, then?"

"Pray God, not that; yet I fear something, Captain Ahab. Is not this harpoon for 65 the White Whale?"

"For the white fiend! But now for the barbs; thou must make them thyself, man. Here are my razors—the best of steel; here, and make the barbs sharp as the needle-sleet of the Icy Sea."

For a moment, the old blacksmith eyed the razors as though he would fain not 70 use them.

"Take them, man, I have no need for them; for I now neither shave, sup, nor pray till—but here—to work!"

Fashioned at last into an arrowy shape, and welded by Perth to the shank, the steel soon pointed the end of the iron; and as the blacksmith was about giving the 75 barbs their final heat, prior to tempering them, he cried to Ahab to place the water-cask near.

"No, no—no water for that; I want it of the true death-temper. Ahoy, there! Tashtego, Queequeg, Daggoo! What say ye, pagans! Will ye give me as much blood as will cover this barb?" holding it high up. A cluster of dark nods replied, Yes. 80 Three punctures were made in the heathen flesh, and the White Whale's barbs were then tempered.

"Ego non baptizo te in nomine patris, sed in nomine diaboli!" deliriously howled Ahab, as the malignant iron scorchingly devoured the baptismal blood.

1. "Perth" is
    A. the ship's blacksmith.
    B. Captain Ahab's birth name.
    C. another name for the Parsee.
    D. the type of spear the blacksmith is hammering.

2. "Mother Carey's chickens" is a sailor's term for storm petrels, or small sea birds. The metaphor in lines 7-11 likens Perth to
    F. sea birds.
    G. the waves created by a ship.
    H. a ship in transit.
    J. a scar.

3. Which of the following lines best paraphrases line 15, "In no Paradise myself, I am impatient of all misery in others that is not mad"?
    A. Because I am on my way to paradise, I do not deal with crazy people.
    B. Since I am marked for damnation, I have no time people who merely think themselves crazy.
    C. As one who suffers, I have no patience for people who suffer, but not from madness.
    D. Join me in misery and allow yourself to go mad, where you can endure it.

4. Which word best describes Perth's willingness to help Ahab?
    A. cautious
    B. calculating
    C. eager
    D. ecstatic

5. The actions of the Parsee make it seem as though he
    F. is watching the blacksmith to ensure that Ahab's harpoon is made properly.
    G. is comfortable or perhaps familiar with the unholy ceremony taking place.
    H. fears for his life amid a crew of heathens and an insane captain.
    J. knows the blacksmith personally because the Parsee bows to him.

6. Ahab wants a harpoon made of
    A. nails from race-horse shoes because it is the hardest steel available.
    B. melted mast screws, because Ahab needs the razors for shaving.
    C. musket barrels and iron rods, for their tolerance to high heat.
    D. melted down gold coins, which he provides in a leather bag.

7. What is the implication of lines 69-72?
    F. Ahab will forego everyday activities until the white whale is harpooned.
    G. Ahab intends to refrain from normal behavior of a ship captain.
    H. Everyday actions are not important to Ahab any more.
    J. Donating the razors is Ahab's main contribution to the barb-making.

8. Ahab's insistence that Perth repair his wounded head (lines 26-34) is a metaphor that suggests:
    F. Ahab will retire soon, because is he aged and wrinkled and wishes to end his suffering.
    G. Wise blacksmiths know that the human skull cannot withstand the heat of a forge.
    H. Ahab's wound is not merely physical; his mind is wounded, and he is irreparably insane.
    J. Perth serves a role as the ship's counselor, but knows that Ahab is beyond help.

9. What substance does Ahab use to temper the barbs of his newly forged harpoon?
    A. sweat from the Parsee
    B. saltwater from the sea
    C. blood from the pagans
    D. oil from the white whale

10. The imagery used in this scene is suggestive of
    F. a witch's lair
    G. a factory floor.
    H. a blacksmith's forge.
    J. a biblical hell.

Book Two

Vocabulary
Power Plus
for the
ACT
Vocabulary,
Reading, and Writing
Exercises for High Scores

Lesson Nineteen

1. **mellifluous** (mə li′ flōō wəs) *adj.* having a rich, smoothly flowing sound
The singer's *mellifluous* voice contributed to the relaxed atmosphere of the lounge.
syn: harmonious   *ant: strident; discordant*

2. **epicurean** (e pi kyū′ rē ən) *adj.* taking pleasure in food and drink
The *epicurean* chef taught his students not only how to cook food, but also how to enjoy it.
syn: hedonistic; gourmet

3. **oeuvre** (ĕ′ vrə or ōō vrə) *n.* the complete work of an artist, composer, or writer
Shakespeare's *oeuvre* is one of the most respected groups of literary works ever written.
syn: canon

4. **arbiter** (är′ bə tər) *n.* a person with the ability to resolve a disagreement; a judge
The principal ended the conflict by acting as an *arbiter* between the two angry students.

5. **verdant** (vər′ dənt) *adj.* fresh and green, referring to plant life
The *verdant* landscape reminded the O'Connells of their native Ireland so much that they decided to build a home there.
syn: lush   *ant: arid; sere*

6. **vagary** (vā′ gə rē) *n.* unpredictable action or behavior
Kristin's *vagaries* prevented her from holding a job as an air traffic controller.
syn: whim; caprice

7. **vacuous** (va′ kyə wəs) *adj.* lacking intelligence; empty of reason
The student's *vacuous* expression revealed his failure to study for the test.
syn: empty-headed   *ant: brilliant; shrewd*

8. **attrition** (ə tri´ shən) *n.* a wearing down over time
The company faced a severe *attrition* of its stock price because of bad publicity.
syn: erosion   *ant: buildup; accretion*

9. **archetype** (är´ ki ūp) *n.* a prototype or original model
The *archetype* for the first airplane was only a toy model, but it has led to modern jets and supersonic fighter planes.
syn: model   *ant: product*

10. **approbation** (a prə bā´ shən) *n.* formal approval of an act
The president gave his *approbation* for the rescue of ten citizens who were being held hostage at a foreign embassy.
syn: authorization   *ant: disapproval; opprobrium*

11. **burgeon** (bər´ jən) *v.* to grow, expand, or bloom
Increased colonization caused the island city to *burgeon*.
syn: swell   *ant: shrink; diminish*

12. **commensurate** (kə men´ sər it) *adj.* an equal measure; corresponding in size and measurement
Though Margie and Liz attended different universities, they received *commensurate* educations.
syn: equivalent; comparable   *ant: unequal*

13. **confluence** (kän´ flōō ənts) *n.* a meeting or gathering together
The United Nations General Assembly is a *confluence* of world thought.
syn: convergence; concourse   *ant: divergence*

14. **coup** (kōō) *n.* a surprising, brilliant, and usually successful act
The rebels planned a *coup* to overthrow the current Prime Minister and install a new leader.
syn: plot

15. **secular** (se´ kyə lər) *adj.* not spiritual or religious; worldly
Many religions warn of the dangers of the *secular* world because they believe it is full of sin.
syn: earthly   *ant: religious*

Exercise I

Words in Context

From the list below, supply the words needed to complete the paragraph. Some words will not be used.

arbiter   vacuous   burgeon   commensurate   vagary   secular

A.   As the terrorist threat _____ each year in the United States, citizens must raise their vigilance to _____ levels. Citizens must also hinder terrorist intelligence-gathering capabilities by implementing small irregularities in their day-to-day routines. These intentional _____ in behavior will prevent terrorists from determining the best time to attack. We must learn to vary concentrations of people, control the distribution of work schedules, and otherwise keep terrorists as _____ as possible about our daily routines.

From the list below, supply the words needed to complete the paragraph. Some words will not be used.

archetype   verdant   attrition   confluence

epicurean   mellifluous   coup

B.   Tonia closed her eyes to concentrate better on the _____ sounds of the mambo orchestra playing at Anconia's Night Club. She heard only what emanated through the rear wall. She would stand next to the wall, close her eyes, and imagine that she was a member of the _____ clientele feasting at the glass tables in Anconia's impressive ballroom. Just a week earlier, Tonia had met Anconia's doorman after the club had closed for the night, and he was nice enough to allow her inside for a look. The walls around the dance floor and dining area were _____ with dangling, subtropical plants, and the dance floor sparkled even though the club was fifty years old. Impressed, Tonia realized how Anconia's provided a place for the _____ of the wealthy and the famous.

From the list below, supply the words needed to complete the paragraph. Some words will not be used.

oeuvre	arbiter	attrition	archetype
approbation	coup	secular	vagary

C.   J.T. Fleming, donning a beret and sitting in a raised, wooden folding chair, seemed to be a perfect _____ of the Hollywood director. With two science fiction blockbusters in his _____ that had made over $1 billion worldwide, Fleming had come to enjoy the _____ of all his investors, until his latest production.

In a departure from _____ films, Fleming now wanted to make a masterpiece based on religious themes. Afraid that the film might offend many patrons, the investors began to plot a[n] _____ against Fleming and slowly pulled their funding for the project. The consequent lawsuits over the contracts between the studio and the investors kept _____ working for months determining who owed money, and the lengthy delay in production caused a[n] _____ of interest in the film, eventually leading it to open poorly at the box office.

Exercise II

Sentence Completion

Complete the sentence in a way that shows you understand the meaning of the italicized vocabulary word.

1. Before taking the case to court, the companies brought in an *arbiter* to...

2. The *epicurean* restaurant owner paled when her doctor told her that...

3. To prove that he was not as *vacuous* as everyone thought, Gene...

4. Bonnie and Doug opted for a *secular* wedding because...

5. If the deadly bacteria in the dish *burgeon* uncontrollably, the scientist will...

6. The *confluence* of the rivers enabled...

7. Roslyn found it easy drift off to the *mellifluous* sounds of...

8. Tycho's *verdant* front yard resembled...

9. Picasso's *oeuvre* was the topic of conversation during...

10. Unlike the traditional *archetype* of the mad scientist, Hans looks and behaves more like...

11. The vice-president of the corporation gave his *approbation* to finance the...

12. Had the *coup* against Lincoln succeeded completely, the country now known as the United States would...

13. Though Kaneka and Robin grew up in different places, they had *commensurate* levels of...

14. The *vagaries* and unpredictability of the hurricane...

15. The increase in student *attrition* in the advanced class caused...

Exercise III

Roots, Prefixes, and Suffixes

Study the entries and answer the questions that follow.

The root *cogn* means "to know."
The root *ped* means "foot."
The root *ject* means "to throw."
The prefix *inter* means "between"
The prefix *in* means "not."
The prefix *de* means "down."
The prefix *im* means "on, against."

A. Using literal translations as guidance, define the following words without using a dictionary:

1. interject   4. impediment
2. incognito   5. pedestrian
3. dejected   6. cognitive

B. If you need foot surgery, you will probably go to a[n]
_____.
An insect that seems to have a thousand legs is called a[n]
_____.

C. Bullets, arrows, and rocks that are thrown from catapults are types of _____.
If *pro* means "before," then a *prognosis* is knowledge about
_____.

D. List all the words that you can think of that contain the roots *cogn*, *ped*, and *ject*.

Exercise IV

Inference

Complete the sentences by inferring information about the italicized word from its context.

A.   If you paint your house a *verdant* green, your neighbors might tell you…

B.   One explanation for the *confluence* of pigeons and robins on the street is…

C.   A good reason for peasants to organize a *coup* against their ruler is…

Exercise V

Writing

Here is a writing prompt similar to the one you will find on the essay writing portion of the ACT.

The Age of Information has brought countless advancements, perhaps, but it also guarantees individuals a digital history, which might not be a good thing. Imagine interviewing for a high-powered job one day only to be turned down because your prospective employers find pictures of you being foolish on your social networking page, or read comments you made on a political website. The things you have posted online are there forever, or must be assumed to be permanent since you have no control over what people do with data you post, even if that means simply leaving it posted for eternity.

What do you recommend to friends who express interest in posting pictures or text, publically, on the Internet? How would you advocate it or condemn it? Include at least three reasons why you do or do not support it.

Thesis: Write a *one-sentence* response to the above assignment. Make certain this single sentence offers a clear statement of your position.

Example: Images or personal data should never be posted on public Internet sites because they may be seen by and judged negatively by someone.

_____

_____

Organizational Plan: List at least three subtopics you will use to support your main idea. This list is your outline.

1. _____

2. _____

3. _____

Draft: Following your outline, write a good first draft of your essay. Remember to support all your points with examples, facts, references to reading, etc.

Review and Revise: Exchange essays with a classmate. Using the Holistic Scoring Guide on page 229, score your partner's essay (while he or she scores yours). If necessary, rewrite your essay to correct the problems indicated by the essay's score.

Exercise VI

English Practice

Improving Paragraphs

Read the following passage and then choose the best revision for the underlined portions of the paragraph. The questions will require you to make decisions regarding the revision of the reading selection. Some revisions are not of actual mistakes, but will improve the clarity of the writing.

[1]

(1) In 1891, Jay <u>Gould, a wealthy railroad magnate, promised</u>[1] to rebuild a church in Roxbury, new york. (2) <u>As a member of the church he had vowed to build, Gould knew that the previous building had been prone to storms and fires, he pledged to fund stone construction of the church, which is what had recently destroyed the church.</u>[2] (3) <u>Never getting to see the church that was built with his money by his children, he died in 1892, but the church that Gould promised definitely was built.</u>[3]

1. A. NO CHANGE
   B. Gould, who is a wealthy railroad magnate, promised
   C. Gould a wealthy railroad magnate promised
   D. Gould, a wealthy railroad-magnate, promised

2. To improve paragraph 1, sentence 2 should be
   F. deleted.
   G. broken into two sentences.
   H. combined with sentence 1.
   J. left unchanged.

3. Choose the best revision of sentence 3.
   A. Gould died in 1892, but his children fulfilled his promise and built the church.
   B. Before dying in 1892, Gould did not get to see the church built, though his children did, using their inheritance.
   C. The church was not built before Gould died in 1892, but his money was used by his children for the same purpose.
   D. Before his promise was fulfilled, Gould died, and, in 1892, his children rebuilt the church.

[2]

(4) The church just happened to be erected right next to a house that had been built thirty years <u>earlier, next door,</u>[4] and one that Gould's daughter, Helen, <u>fancied</u>.[5] (5) Not long after the church was completed, Helen bought the estate. (6) She named it "Kirkside" for its position adjacent to the neighboring Kirkside Lake. (7) The house was built by Liberty Preston.

4. F. NO CHANGE
   G. earlier
   H. earlier, again, right next door,
   J. earlier—next door—

5. A. NO CHANGE
   B. made fancy
   C. financed
   D. had made fancy

6. Which sentence could be deleted without changing the intent of the paragraph?
   F. Sentence 4
   G. Sentence 5
   H. Sentence 6
   J. Sentence 7

[3]

After <u>Goulds</u>[7] death, his <u>6 children</u>[8] took up the cause and even financed the project. Construction began in 1893 for the early English Gothic-style church built with rough-faced St. Lawrence marble. The church was completed in 1894 and dedicated to <u>Gould the Jay Gould Memorial Reformed Church</u>.[9]

7. A. NO CHANGE
   B. Goulds's
   C. Goulds'
   D. Gould's

8. F. NO CHANGE
   G. 6 children
   H. six children
   J. six childrens

9. A. NO CHANGE
   B. Gould and named the Jay Gould Memorial Reformed Church
   C. Gould, the Jay Gould Memorial Reformed Church
   D. Gould; The Jay Gould Memorial Reformed Church

[4]

When she died in 1938, the beauty of Kirkside became available to many other people besides Helen.[10] Twelve acres of the estate have since become Kirkside Park, a center of activity in Roxbury. Helen's brother donated the house to the Reformed Church of America as a retirement home for clerics and their families. Eventually, the home were opened[11] to elderly persons of all denominations.

10. F. NO CHANGE
   G. When she died in 1938, Kirkside allowed its beauty out to everybody—not just Helen.
   H. When the death of Helen allowed the beauty of Kirkside to become available in 1938.
   J. When Helen died in 1938, the beauty of Kirkside became available to many other people.

11. A. NO CHANGE
   B. was opened
   C. opened up
   D. is open

[5]

There are people who claim that Jay Gould was a robber baron, and that he became the ninth richest man in the world by exploiting cheap labor and creating monopolies. Gould did once bail Boss Tweed, the most notoriously corrupt politician in the history of New York, out of prison. Other historians say thats[12] not right and that Gould was a regular businessman.

12. F. NO CHANGE
    G. that wasn't
    H. that's
    J. that isn't

13. Which, if any of the paragraphs, should be deleted entirely from the passage?
    A. paragraph 2
    B. paragraph 3
    C. paragraph 4
    D. paragraph 5

14. Which of the following suggestions would improve the organization of the passage?
    F. Exchange paragraph 4 with paragraph 2.
    G. Exchange paragraph 4 with paragraph 3.
    H. Exchange paragraph 1 with paragraph 4.
    J. Exchange paragraph 3 with paragraph 2.

15. Choose the most appropriate title for the passage.
    A. Two Parks for the Price of One
    B. Legacy of a Robber Baron
    C. Jay Gould's Kirkside Home
    D. The Gift of Gould

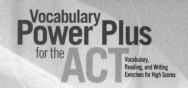

Vocabulary
Power Plus
for the
ACT
Vocabulary,
Reading, and Writing
Exercises for High Scores

Lesson Twenty

1. **insouciant** (in sōō´ sē ənt) *adj.* not concerned; free from care
Jenna's *insouciant* attitude made her easy to befriend.
syn: nonchalant   *ant: worried*

2. **static** (sta´ tik) *adj.* without force or movement; stationary
The old truck remained *static* in the front yard because it was out of gasoline.
syn: immobile; inert   *ant: dynamic*

3. **stipulate** (sti´ pyə lāt) *v.* to specify a required part of an agreement
The developer *stipulated* that before construction could begin, the homeowners must first provide a down payment.
syn: require

4. **zeitgeist** (zīt´ gīst) *n.* the general spirit of the time
Some consider the *zeitgeist* of the 1960s to be one of moral decay, while others see it as a time of reform.

5. **proliferate** (prə li´ fə rāt) *v.* to grow or reproduce rapidly
The plant food enabled Bob's irises to *proliferate* throughout the flower bed.
syn: multiply   *ant: diminish*

6. **tenet** (te´ nət) *n.* a belief or principle held to be true
Belief in the Holy Trinity is one of the main *tenets* of Catholicism.
syn: cornerstone; creed

7. **ruminate** (rōō´ mə nāt) *v.* to think deeply or repeatedly
The great philosopher could often be found *ruminating* over the question of death.
syn: ponder; reflect

8. **vigilant** (vi´ jə lent) *adj.* alert at all times; watchful
The family's watchdog remained *vigilant* during the day, but he fell into a deep sleep at night.
syn: alert   *ant: oblivious*

9. **dissident** (di′ sə dənt) *n.* someone who disagrees
The *dissidents* of the proposed welfare bill staged a protest.
syn: renegade   *ant: supporter*

10. **petulant** (pe′ chə lənt) *adj.* rude in speech or behavior; peevish
Mike's *petulant* remarks toward his boss earned him a demotion and a cut in pay.
syn: contemptuous   *ant: original*

11. **derivative** (də ri′ və tiv) *n.* not the original; coming from another source
The modern English word "engine" is a *derivative* of the Latin word "ingenium."
syn: offspring; branch

12. **accolade** (a′ kə lād) *n.* an award or honor
The reporter received *accolades* for her newest article that uncovered a serious money-laundering scandal.
syn: kudos; recognition   *ant: opprobrium*

13. **demur** (di mər′) *v.* to disapprove or to take exception
Martin *demurred* when Sandy suggested that they spend Friday evening at the ballet.
syn: object; disagree   *ant: agree; acquiesce*

14. **limpid** (lim′ pəd) *adj.* transparent; clear
The warm, *limpid* waters of the Aegean Sea provide excellent snorkeling opportunities.
       ant: murky

15. **invidious** (in vi′ dē əs) *adj.* tending to cause discontent, harm, or resentment; offensively unfair
The *invidious* book caused a huge controversy over implications that a leading presidential candidate committed a crime.
syn: malicious   *ant: conciliatory*

Exercise I

Words in Context

From the list below, supply the words needed to complete the paragraph. Some words will not be used.

limpid	proliferate	tenet	ruminate	accolade
zeitgeist	stipulate	insouciant	static	dissident

A. Thirty years of saving money finally paid off when Vernita found the cottage of her dreams on the coast of Maine—or so she thought. Despite a handful of local _____, the Clifftown Historical Society approved the sale of the property, but not before they _____ one important factor: the new owner must keep the windmill in operating condition because it had been a landmark of the town for generations. Shrugging off the windmill as a minor concern, Vernita seized the opportunity to purchase the lot. Six months later, Vernita learned why the _____ of the cottage's original era included a rigorous work ethic.

   The problems began when she walked outside on a breezy morning and noticed the _____ blades of the windmill, despite the considerable breeze. The shaft to the millstones had broken, and its repair required nearly two thousand dollars and three weeks of toiling for her and two paid workmen. Two days after completing the repairs, the well began to pump a muddy, undrinkable liquid instead of its usual cool, _____ spring water. While contractors dug a new well, Vernita discovered that mold and insects had _____ in the dank basement. The unending problems caused Vernita to _____ on why she had ever bought the house. She had always believed in one _____: sometimes, people just have to know when to quit, and Vernita also missed the _____ life that she had while renting someone else's property. Three months later, Vernita moved back into a condominium.

From the list below, supply the words needed to complete the paragraph. Some words will not be used.

static	accolade	vigilant	petulant
invidious	demur	derivative	stipulate

B. "Keep your _____ comments to yourself," said Kyle. "They're not going to help matters. We needed a pilot, and Brad was the only team member who even came close."

Lee Ann stopped complaining, but she thought again of how she foolishly _____ to Logan's half-witted escape plan, which she felt could cause _____ harm or even death. They were to grab the canisters, sneak out of the compound, run through the jungle, and steal one of the two old cargo planes on the dirt runway. Two team members had already been wounded, and Brad wasn't about to win any _____ for his abilities to get the dilapidated machine off the ground.

"This plane's no good!" screamed Brad. "The left engine must need maintenance!"

"Let's try the other plane before the alarm sounds!" yelled Lee Ann. The team grabbed what little gear they had left, exited the plane, and hurried across the tarmac. Knowing that Benedito's security force would soon descend on them, the Americans remained _____ even as they scrambled to the other plane with their gear. While boarding, Kyle flinched when he looked beyond the flaps and caught sight of motorcycles entering the runway from the access road to the compound.

"Fire it up! Now!" yelled Kyle as he crawled over the team and landed with a thud in the primitive cockpit. "And check the canisters!"

Lee Ann checked. Luckily, the two quart-sized stainless steel canisters were intact and sealed; after all, one milligram of Prenitite would be more than enough to stop the hearts of everyone on the plane. A[n] _____ of the Prentonica seed, Prenitite was the number one item on every terrorist's wishlist.

Exercise II

Sentence Completion

Complete the sentence in a way that shows you understand the meaning of the italicized vocabulary word.

1. My moral *tenets* prevent me from helping you to...

2. Your *petulant* attitude toward our clients has cost the company...

3. Displeased with the mayor's decision, several *dissidents*...

4. The tide pools are so *limpid* that you can see...

5. The reformists decided that the present *zeitgeist* did not...

6. The *vigilant* soldier on night watch heard the...

7. The Church declared that the work of art was too *invidious* so it was displayed for one day before...

8. As landmines *proliferate*, special United Nations teams...

9. The mayor realized his mistake when the *insouciant* toll bridge operator...

10. Chloe received *accolades* for exposing the corporate cover-up, but then her boss...

11. I *demured* when asked to...

12. From the Greek root "chron," we get the *derivative* word...

13. If you *ruminate* too much before you swing the bat, you'll definitely...

14. I would have bought the car, but the dealer *stipulated* that...

15. Vaughn assumed that the *static* pendulum meant that the clock was...

Exercise III

Roots, Prefixes, and Suffixes

Study the entries and answer the questions that follow.

The roots *cord* and *card* mean "heart" or "mind."
The roots *quis* and *quir* mean "to seek."
The prefix *ac* means "towards."
The prefix *in* means "into."
The prefix *cata* means "down" or "thoroughly"
The root *tonia* means, "paralysis."
The root *clysm* means "flood, disaster."

A. *Using literal translations as guidance, define the following words without using a dictionary:*

    1. inquisitive   4. catatonia
    2. discordant   5. cataclysm
    3. acquisitive   6. cordial

B. An agreement among nations to stop a particular behavior is sometimes called a[n] _____.
Explain why the word *catapult* would use the "to put down" form of *cata*. Repeat the process for the word *catalog*.

C. The purpose of an *inquisition* is to _____.
If the prefix *re* means "again," what is the literal translation of *record* (verb form)?

D. List as many words as you can that contain the roots *cord*, *quis*, or *cata*.

Exercise IV

Inference

Complete the sentences by inferring information about the italicized word from its context.

A. Rumors of executives stealing from the company continue to *proliferate* because…

B. If the political *dissident* does not publicly retract his statement, the dictator might…

C. If the pond is no longer *limpid* after the factory begins production, you might assume that…

Exercise V

Critical Reading

Below is a reading passage followed by several multiple-choice questions similar to the ones you will encounter on the ACT. Carefully read the passage and choose the best answer to each of the questions.

From 1804 to 1806, Meriwether Lewis and William Clark led the first official overland expedition to the Pacific Coast. The following passage is one day of journal entries for Lewis and Clark on the day of April 20, 1806, about one month into the return trip. The expedition party is near the Columbia River, which forms the current border between Washington and Oregon.

Sunday, April 20, 1806 (Captain Lewis):

Some frost this morning. The Eneeshur and Skilloots are much better clad than they were last fall; their men have generally leggings, moccasins, and large robes; many of them wear shirts of the same form with those of the Shoshone Chopunnish,
5 highly ornamented with porcupine quills. The dress of their women differs very little from those of the great rapids and above. Their children frequently wear robes of the large grey squirrel skins, those of the men and women are principally deer skins, some wolf, elk, bighorn, and buffalo; the latter they procure from the nations who sometimes visit the Missouri. Indeed a considerable proportion of their
10 wearing apparel is purchased from their neighbors to the northwest in exchange for pounded fish, copper, and beads. At present, the principal village of the Eneeshur is below the falls on the north side of the river. One other village is above the falls on the south side and another a few miles above on the north side. The first consists of

nineteen, the second of eleven, and the third of five lodges. Their houses, like those
15 of the Skilloots, have their floors on the surface of the ground, but are formed of
sticks and covered with mats and straw. They are large and contain usually several
families each. For fuel, they use straw, small willows, and the southern wood. They
use the silk grass in manufacturing their fishing nets and bags, and the bear grass
and cedar bark are employed in forming a variety of articles. They are poor, dirty,
20 proud, haughty, inhospitable, parsimonious, and faithless in every respect; nothing
but our numbers, I believe, prevents their attempting to murder us at this moment.

This morning I was informed that the natives had pilfered six tomahawks and
a knife from the party in the course of the last night. I spoke to the chief on this
subject. He appeared angry with his people and addressed them, but the property
25 was not restored. One horse which I had purchased and paid for yesterday, and
which could not be found when I ordered the horses into close confinement
yesterday, I was now informed had been gambled away by the rascal who had sold
it to me and had been taken away by a man of another nation. I therefore took the
goods back from this fellow. I purchased a gun from the chief for which I gave him
30 two elk skins. In the course of the day, I obtained two other indifferent horses for
which I gave an extravagant price. I found that I should get no more horses and
therefore resolved to proceed tomorrow morning with those which I had and to
convey the baggage in two small canoes that the horses could not carry. For this
purpose, I had a load made up for seven horses; the eighth Bratton was compelled to
35 ride as he was yet unable to walk. I bartered my elk skins, old irons, and two canoes
for beads. One of the canoes for which they would give us but little, I had cut up
for fuel. These people have yet a large quantity of dried fish on hand, yet they will
not let us have any but for an exorbitant price. We purchased two dogs and some
shappellel from them. I had the horses grazed until evening and then picketed and
40 hobbled them within the limits of our camp. I ordered the indians from our camp
this evening and informed them that if I caught them attempting to purloin any
article from us, I would beat them severely. They went off in rather a bad humor,
and I directed the party to examine their arms and be on their guard. They stole two
spoons from us in the course of the day. The Scaddals, Squan-nan-os, Shan-wah-
45 purrs, and Shallattas reside to the northwest of these people, and depend on hunting
deer and elk and trade with these people for their pounded fish.

Sunday, April 20, 1806 (Captain Clark):

This morning very cold; hills covered with snow. I showed the natives what I
had to give for their horses and attempted to purchase them. They informed me that
50 they would not sell any horses to me, that their horses were at a long ways off and
they would not trade them. My offer was a blue robe, a calico shirt, a handkerchief,
five parcels of paint, a knife, a wampum moon, four braces of ribbon, a piece of
brass, and about six braces of yellow beads; and to that amount for what I had, I
also offered my large blue blanket for one, my coat, sword and plume—none of
55 which seemed to entice those people to give horses if they had any. They sat in their
huts, which are mats supported on poles without fire. At night, when they wish a
light, they burn dry straw and some small, dry willows. They speak different from
those below, and have but little to eat. Some roots and dried fish are to be found in
their houses. I am half frozen at this inhospitable village, which is moved from its

60 position above the falls to one below, and contains nineteen large houses. A village is also established on the other side, immediately above the falls. All the natives who were established above the falls for some distance have moved. Those people are much better dressed than they were at the time we went down the river. They have all new deer, elk, ibex, goat, and wolf skin robes, their children have also the large
65 squirrel skin robes. Many of them have leggings and moccasins, all of which they procure from the indians at a distance in exchange for their pounded fish and beads. They also purchase silk grass, of which they make their nets and sails for taking fish. They also purchase bear grass and many other things for their fish. Those people gave me roots and berries prepared in different ways, for which I gave some small
70 articles in return. Great numbers of skimming nets on their houses. Those people are poor and kind of dirty and indolent. They wear their hair loose and flowing; the men cut in the forward, which the Skilloots do not.

I could not procure a single horse from those people, during this day, at any price. They offered me two for two kettles, of which we could not spare. I used
75 every artifice decent and even false statements to induce those poor devils to sell me horses. In the evening, two different men offered to sell me three horses, which they informed me were a little distance off and they would bring them immediately. Those two persons, as I found, went immediately off up the river to their tribe without any intention to find or sell their horses. A little before sunset, three men
80 arrived from some distance above and informed me that they came to see me. At sunset, finding no probability of Captain Lewis' arrival, I packed up the articles and took them into the lodge in which I lay last night. Great numbers of those people gathered around me to smoke. I gave them two pipes and lay down in the back part of the house with Sgt. P. and the men with our arms situated as to be ready in case
85 of any alarm. Those poor people appear entirely harmless—I purchased a dog and some wood with a little pounded fish and shappellels. Made a fire on the rocks and cooked the dogs on which the men breakfasted and dined. Wind was hard all day, cold and from the northwest.

1. Lewis' party lacks enough horses to carry all the equipment, so Lewis
   A. hires Skilloots to help him carry the gear.
   B. burns anything that he cannot carry.
   C. purchases eight more horses.
   D. transports the equipment in canoes.

2. One of Lewis's horses does not carry equipment because
   F. it is Captain Bratton's expensive show horse.
   G. the equipment is placed in canoes.
   H. the horse is stubborn and refuses to cross the river.
   J. it must carry Bratton, an injured member of the party.

3. As used in line 40, *hobbled* most nearly means
   A. limped.
   B. broke the legs of to prevent escape.
   C. tied the legs of to restrict movement.
   D. staggered, as though suffering from leg wounds.

4. Which information can be inferred from line 81?
   F. Lewis and Clark are lost somewhere near the Pacific coast.
   G. The natives treat Clark better than they treat Lewis.
   H. Lewis and Clark are not together in the same camp.
   J. Lewis is waiting for Clark to arrive.

5. As used in line 75, *artifice* most nearly means
   A. an obvious lie.
   B. a crafty maneuver.
   C. a threatening statement.
   D. a false promise.

6. To purchase clothing from other nations, the Eneeshur and Skilloot Indians used
   F. kettles.
   G. shappellel.
   H. pounded fish.
   J. calico.

7. Which statement is *false* at the time the journal entries were written?
   A. Lewis and Clark had not previously met the Eneeshur and Skilloot Indians.
   B. One Eneeshur village contained nineteen lodges.
   C. The expedition teams needed horses.
   D. The expedition teams ate dogs.

8. Lewis and Clark do not agree
   F. on the general physical appearance of the natives.
   G. that there is a need for more horses.
   H. on the level of threat posed by the natives.
   J. that the Eneeshur and Skilloots are fishermen.

9. Which choice best describes the change in tone between the entries?
   A. Clark is not as impersonal as Lewis.
   B. Clark is more detached and impersonal than Lewis.
   C. Clark does not refer to himself in the first person.
   D. Lewis is spirited and lively, while Clark is serious and solemn.

10. In their journal entries, neither Lewis nor Clark mentions
    F. the weather conditions.
    G. the locations of the Eneeshur villages.
    H. the characteristics of the native dwellings.
    J. the distance the party plans to travel the next day.

Vocabulary
Power Plus
for the ACT
Vocabulary,
Reading, and Writing
Exercises for High Scores

Book Two

Lesson Twenty-One

1. **august** (o gəst´) *adj.* marked by grandeur and awe
    The coronation of the queen was an *august* occasion that was full of pomp and circumstance.
    syn: regal; magnificent   *ant: pedestrian; common*

2. **ancillary** (an´ si lə rē) *adj.* subsidiary; providing assistance
    The senior executive of the firm hired an *ancillary* worker to do his filing and typing.

3. **semblance** (sem´ bləns) *n.* an outward likeness in form or appearance
    The suspect's alibi was only a partial *semblance* of the truth.
    syn: similarity; copy

4. **autodidact** (o tō dī´ dakt) *n.* a self-taught person
    With accomplishments in law, politics, and literature, Abe Lincoln is perhaps the most famous *autodidact* in American history.
    syn: self-educated

5. **asinine** (as´ ə nīn) *adj.* exhibiting poor judgment or intelligence
    Jonah revealed his *asinine* tendencies when he rudely insulted the rabbi.
    syn: foolish; boorish; silly   *ant: sagacious*

6. **albeit** (ôl bē´ ət) *conj.* although; even though
    It was rainy and miserable all summer, *albeit* good for the crops.

7. **conduit** (kän´ dōō ət) *n.* a means by which something is transmitted
    The telephone wire must be plugged into the *conduit* for the computer to connect to the Internet.
    syn: channel

8. **philatelist** (fə lat´ əl ist) *n.* one who collects stamps
    As a prominent *philatelist*, Dr. James has over ten thousand stamps in his collection.

9. **indefatigable** (in di fat´ i gə bəl) *adj.* tireless; incapable of being fatigued
    Dave was so passionate about his work that he seemed almost *indefatigable* to the rest of the group.
    ant: exhausted

10. **martyr** (mär´ tər) *n.* one who suffers or sacrifices for a cause
Martin Luther King became a *martyr* for the civil rights movement when an assassin killed him.

11. **indiscretion** (in dis kresh´ ən) *n.* a minor misdeed
If it is scandalous enough, a single *indiscretion* can cost a politician his or her career.
syn: peccadillo; transgression

12. **osmosis** (äz mō´ səs) *n.* a gradual, often unconscious, process of absorption
Living in a foreign country allowed Jerry to learn its language by *osmosis*.

13. **picayune** (pi kē yōōn´) *adj.* of very little value; trivial; inconsequential
Mike's *picayune* collection of toy trucks had more sentimental value than the few dollars it would get at auction.
syn: worthless; cheap   *ant: valuable*

14. **dossier** (dos´ yā) *n.* a file of detailed information on a person or subject
The police had a large *dossier* on the man accused of the theft.
syn: record

15. **behest** (bi hest´) *n.* a command or urgent request
Tyler grudgingly obeyed his mother's *behest* to come home early after the school dance.
syn: demand

Exercise I

Words in Context

From the list below, supply the words needed to complete the paragraph. Some words will not be used.

dossier	semblance	picayune	albeit
august	indefatigable	philatelist	behest

A.   Like many residents of Crystal Point, Janine walked to the beach every evening to witness the _____ beauty of the sun setting over the Pacific. The white dunes were the best place to experience the beautiful event, _____ several barges on the horizon diminished the view. They were a[n] _____ detail to Janine; it would require more than a few dots on the horizon to distract her from the blazing sky. Today, as Janine approached the water, she was amused to find a large mound of sand that had a vague _____ of a whale. The Williards must have visited the beach; they have three _____ children who readily spend entire days creating sand sculptures.

From the list below, supply the words needed to complete the paragraph. Some words will not be used.

asinine	**conduit**	**osmosis**	**august**
autodidact	**indiscretion**	**behest**	

B. Alicia knew that it was _____ to wait until the night before the deadline to write her term paper. Her teacher had accepted a late paper in the past, but Alicia recognized that such _____ would not be ignored this time because it was the end of the grading period.

Luckily for her, Alicia was a(n) _____ who spent her free time reading about the subject of her paper. Having parents who were experts in the field also helped; raised by two historians, Alicia had learned more about history through _____ than she could ever hope to acquire in a classroom.

From the list below, supply the words needed to complete the paragraph. Some words will not be used.

conduit	**semblance**	**dossier**	**philatelist**
ancillary	**behest**	**martyr**	

C. At the FBI Director's _____, Special Agent Ford compiled a[n] _____ on Caroline Polk, including a list of charges, previous warrants, and a psychological profile. No, it was not every day that a stamp thief made it to the most-wanted list, but Polk had simply gone too far when she burglarized the stamp collection of Terry Moore, a well known _____ and, more important, a United States Senator. Identifying the suspect had taken only hours; thanks to some _____ guidance from the local police department's homicide unit, investigators found Polk's fingerprints all over the heating _____ that she used to enter the Senator's house. Polk's fingerprints were on record, largely because she was the only person in the country currently wanted for the grand theft of precious stamps. The Bureau had declined to arrest Polk in the past, for she was known to be armed, and few agents were willing to become _____ to the cause of stamp collecting.

Exercise II

Sentence Completion

Complete the sentence in a way that shows you understand the meaning of the italicized vocabulary word.

1. Ursula was reminded of her past *indiscretions* every time she…

2. "Your *dossier* reads like a novel," said Dr. Isano as he…

3. Your concerns are too *picayune* for me to…

4. The weather was sunny and clear, *albeit*…

5. If the hospital suffers a blackout, *ancillary* services are…

6. Phoebe felt out of place at the *august* induction ceremony because…

7. The highlight of the *philatelist's* collection is a…

8. The broken underground gas *conduit* caused a mass…

9. Thanks to four cups of coffee, the *indefatigable* Elizabeth can finish…

10. Ivan was brave, but becoming a *martyr* was…

11. At the Admiral's *behest*, Petty Officer Young gave the order to…

12. Audrey's *asinine* decision to put foil in the microwave resulted in…

13. As if by *osmosis*, the rambunctious hockey fans turned the docile Freddy…

14. Living far from civilization and schools, the *autodidact* had to…

15. The shoddy reality show didn't bear any *semblance* to…

Exercise III

Roots, Prefixes, and Suffixes

Study the entries and answer the questions that follow.

The roots *cap, capt, cept* and *cip* mean "to take" or "to seize."
The roots *grad* and *gress* mean "step" or "to go."
The prefix *inter* means "between," "among," or "in the presence of."

A. *Using literal translations as guidance, define the following words without using a dictionary:*
    1. regress   4. precept
    2. degrade   5. captivate
    3. digress   6. capacious

B. Police will use their cars to _____ a driver who flees the scene of a crime.
    If the prefix *e* means "out," then the literal translation for *egress* is

    _____.

C. The root *mit* means "to send." What is the appropriate word to describe a radio signal that fades in and out, causing periods of silence between audible transmissions?
    The root *rog* means "to ask." What would you call a formal questioning of someone who is present, and expected, to answer the questions?

D. List all the words you can think of that contain the roots *cap, capt, cip,* or *cept.*

E. List all the words you can think of that begin with the prefix *inter.*

Exercise IV

Inference

Complete the sentences by inferring information about the italicized word from its context.

A. The FBI might compile a *dossier* on someone who...

B. If the *autodidact* did not have access to a library, she might not...

C. Since the *ancillary* forces failed to arrive in time, the battalion defending the fort...

Exercise V

Writing

Here is a writing prompt similar to the one you will find on the essay writing portion of the ACT.

> Despite a great deal of discussion about global climate change, there is relatively little talk about what changes the world would have to make in the event that global warming cannot be stopped, regardless of its cause.
>
> Which, in your opinion, should be the priority: attempting to stop global warming by eliminating the production of greenhouse gasses, or preparing to adapt to a warmed world? Write a speech for your science class that details your argument.

Thesis: Write a *one-sentence* response to the above assignment. Make certain this single sentence offers a clear statement of your position.

Example: Because eliminating greenhouse gas levels seems like an impossible task, humankind should be formulating new technologies that will allow it to adapt to a new environment.

_____

_____

Organizational Plan: List at least three subtopics you will use to support your main idea. This list is your outline.

1. _____

2. _____

3. _____

Draft: Following your outline, write a good first draft of your essay. Remember to support all your points with examples, facts, references to reading, etc.

Review and Revise: Exchange essays with a classmate. Using the Holistic Scoring Guide on page 229, score your partner's essay (while he or she scores yours). If necessary, rewrite your essay to correct the problems noted by your partner.

Exercise VI

English Practice

Identifying Sentence Errors
Identify the errors in the following sentences. Choose the answer that fixes the error. If the sentence contains no error, select answer choice E.

1. Only a few stars <u>were visible last night;</u> because there was a full moon.
   A. NO CHANGE
   B. were visible last night
   C. were visible last night—
   D. were visible last night,

2. By the time the hail started, we had already <u>ran into</u> the library.
   F. NO CHANGE
   G. ran in
   H. run in to
   J. run into

3. <u>Radio stations aired the story about the miracle operation to restore sight to a blind man in every region of the country.</u>
   A. NO CHANGE
   B. Radio stations aired the story about the miracle operation in every region of the country to restore sight to a blind man.
   C. Radio stations in every region of the country aired the story about the miracle operation to restore sight to a blind man.
   D. Radio stations aired the story about the miracle operations to restore sight in every region of the country to a blind man.

4. Jane was <u>already</u> for the prom one hour before her date arrived.
   F. NO CHANGE
   G. allready
   H. all ready
   J. all-ready

5. The university registrar is responsible <u>for scheduling office staff</u>, coordinating the directory of classes and examinations, and assigning classroom facilities.
   A. NO CHANGE
   B. for the scheduling office staff
   C. for scheduling of office staff
   D. for office-staff scheduling

Improving Sentences

The underlined portion of each sentence below contains some flaw. Select the answer that best corrects the flaw.

6. Julie added vegetables to the <u>stew; and then it simmered</u> for twenty minutes before she served it.
    F. stew, and then she allowed it to simmer
    G. stew, simmered it
    H. stew, before it simmered
    J. stew it simmered

7. On Christmas morning, the children <u>had opened all their gifts almost</u> by 6 am.
    A. had opened almost all their gifts
    B. had almost opened all their gifts
    C. had unwrapped all their gifts
    D. had almost opened some presents

8. New research shows that high cholesterol levels are as much a result of heredity <u>as also is a healthy diet and active lifestyle are</u>.
    F. as both a healthy diet and active lifestyle
    G. as are a healthy diet and active lifestyle
    H. as healthy dieting and an active lifestyle are also
    J. also as are a healthy diet and active lifestyle

9. Mary told <u>Ellen that she would need a new outfit to wear to her job interview.</u>
    A. Ellen that she would need a new outfit to wear to the job interview.
    B. Ellen that she needed a new outfit to wear to the job interview.
    C. Ellen that she was going to need a new outfit to wear to the job interview.
    D. Ellen, "You will need a new outfit to wear to the job interview."

10. <u>Neither Anthony nor his brothers like the beach.</u>
    F. Neither Anthony or his brothers likes the beach.
    G. Either Anthony or his brothers like the beach.
    H. Neither Anthony or his brothers like the beach.
    J. Neither Anthony nor his brother's likes the beach.

Vocabulary
Power Plus
for the ACT
Vocabulary,
Reading, and Writing
Exercises for High Scores

REVIEW
Lessons 15–21

Exercise I

Sentence Completion

Choose the best pair of words to complete the sentence. Most choices will fit grammatically and will even make sense logically, but you must choose the pair that best fits the idea of the sentence.

1. The villain perfected his _____ plan to _____ torch from the Statue of Liberty and hold it for ransom.
    A. verbose, burgeon
    B. quixotic, demur
    C. invidious, purloin
    D. august, quell
    E. terse, filibuster

2. The _____ taught herself all the material for a degree in mathematics because she was too _____ to engage in classroom discussions.
    A. tenet, commensurate
    B. plebeian, limpid
    C. philatelist, penitent
    D. archetype, discordant
    E. autodidact, pusillanimous

3. The king quickly arrested all _____ and placed them in prison camps where they were _____ by guards and kept too weak to foment rebellion.
    A. dissidents, subjugated
    B. epicureans, vindicated
    C. zeitgeists, purloined
    D. accolades, connived
    E. lieges, stipulated

4. The city experienced a serious _____ when an explosion at the chemical factory released a(n) _____ cloud that rendered the air lethal to breathe.
   A. dossier, taciturn
   B. semblance, impregnable
   C. exodus, noxious
   D. rabble, mellifluous
   E. scourge, agnostic

5. The rebel leader died during the attempted _____ against the dictator and became a(n) _____ whose death inspired the rebellion.
   A. zephyr, confluence
   B. coup, martyr
   C. tenet, invective
   D. accolade, oeuvre
   E. pandemonium, arbiter

6. The plumber poured a(n) _____ solution down the drain that would _____ the removal of the blockage.
   A. caustic, expedite
   B. static, burgeon
   C. hypercritical, pique
   D. parsimonious, scourge
   E. august, subjugate

7. Until the _____ for international drug trafficking are closed, heroin and cocaine will _____.
   A. raillery, stipulate
   B. dossiers, hurtle
   C. filibusters, pique
   D. fallacies, demur
   E. conduits, proliferate

8. Because Milligan had only a(n) _____ claim on the land, the court-appointed _____ decided the case against him.
   A. tenuous, arbiter
   B. invective, raconteur
   C. penitent, vagary
   D. insouciant, autodidact
   E. secular, liege

Exercise II

Crossword Puzzle

Use the clues to complete the crossword puzzle. The answers consist of vocabulary
words from lessons 15 through 21.

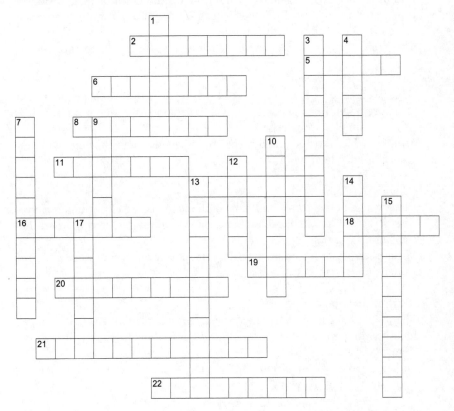

Across
2. ponder
5. hatred
6. rude
8. quiet
11. mediator
13. to steal
16. sarcastic
18. succinct
19. whim

20. to dominate
21. stingy
22. wearing away

Down
1. stately
3. gathering place
4. to displease
7. carefree
9. although

10. wasteful
12. tasteless
13. stamp collector
14. concise
15. advanced
17. not religious

Scoring Guide for the ACT Writing Test

ORGANIZATION

6 = Clearly Competent

The paper is clearly organized around the central point or main idea. The organization may grow from the writer's argument or a slightly predictable structure. Ideas follow a logical order.

The work is **free of surface errors** (grammar, spelling, punctuation, etc.).

5 = Reasonably Competent

The organization of the paper is clear, but not fully implemented. The structure might be predictable. Ideas follow a logical order, but transitions might be simple or obvious.

Minor surface errors are present, but they **do not interfere** with the reader's understanding of the work.

4 = Adequately Competent

The organization of the paper is apparent, but not consistently implemented. The structure is predictable. Some ideas follow a logical order, but transitions are simple and obvious.

Surface errors are present, but they **do not severely interfere** with the reader's understanding.

3 = Nearly Competent

There is evidence of a simple organizational plan. Ideas are grouped logically in parts of the paper, but do not flow logically throughout. Transitions are needed.

Surface errors are **apparent** and **begin to interfere** with the reader's understanding of the work.

2 = Marginally Incompetent

The organizational plan of the paper is obscured by too few details and/or irrelevant details. Some of the ideas are grouped logically in parts of the paper. Transitions are needed or are incorrect.

Surface errors are **frequent and severe enough** to **interfere** with the reader's understanding of the work.

1 = Incompetent

There is no clear organizational plan and/or insufficient material. Ideas are not grouped logically. Transitions are absent.

Surface errors are **frequent** and **extreme,** and **severely interfere** with the reader's understanding of the work.

Scoring Guide for the ACT Writing Test

DEVELOPMENT

6 = Clearly Competent

The **paper takes a position** on the issue and **offers sufficient material** (details, examples, anecdotes, supporting facts, etc.) to create a **complete discussion. Every word and sentence is relevant.** Ideas are **fully supported.** The paper visits **different perspectives** of the argument or addresses **counterarguments** to the writer's position. The paper **focuses** on the argument evoked by the prompt. There is a **clear, purposed,** well developed **introduction** and **conclusion**.

The work is **free of surface errors** (grammar, spelling, punctuation, etc.).

5 = Reasonably Competent

The essay **takes a position** on the issue and **offers sufficient material** for a complete discussion, but the reader is left **with a few unanswered questions.**

Ideas are **supported.** The paper **partially visits different perspectives** of the argument or addresses **counterarguments. Most** of the paper **focuses** on the argument evoked by the prompt. There is **no irrelevant material.** There is a clear **introduction** and **conclusion.**

Minor surface errors are present, but they **do not interfere** with the reader's understanding of the work.

4 = Adequately Competent

The paper **takes a position** on the issue but **does not provide** enough details, examples, or supporting facts for a complete discussion, leaving a **few unanswered questions.** The paper includes **some attention** to **counterarguments** and differing perspectives. **Irrelevant material** is present. **Most** of the paper **focuses** on the topic and the specific argument. **Surface errors** are present, but they **do not severely interfere** with the reader's understanding.

3 = Nearly Competent

The essay **takes a position** on the issue but **does not include** sufficient details, examples, or supporting facts for a discussion. The paper **may include incomplete or unclear counterarguments.** The paper **might repeat** details or rhetoric. The paper focuses on the topic, but **does not maintain** the specific argument.

Surface errors are **apparent** and **begin to interfere** with the reader's understanding of the work.

2 = Marginally Incompetent

The paper **may not take a position** on the issue, or the paper may take a position but **fail to support** it with sufficient details. Examples and ideas are **vague** and **irrelevant**. The paper might **repeat ideas extensively**. The paper **might maintain focus** on the general topic.

Surface errors are **frequent and severe enough** to **interfere** with the reader's understanding of the work.

1 = Incompetent

The paper **might attempt to take a position**, but it **fails to provide** examples, fact, or rhetoric to support the position. The paper may be **repetitious** with **little** or **no focus** on the general topic.

Surface errors are **frequent** and **extreme**, and **severely interfere** with the reader's understanding of the work.

Scoring Guide for the ACT Writing Test

SENTENCE FORMATION AND VARIETY

6 = Clearly Competent
Sentences are **varied**, **complete**, and **assist the reader** in the flow of the discussion.
The work is **free of surface errors** (grammar, spelling, punctuation, etc.).

5 = Reasonably Competent
Sentences are **somewhat varied, generally correct**, and **do not distract** the reader from the flow of the discussion.
Minor surface errors are present, but they **do not interfere** with the reader's understanding of the work.

4 = Adequately Competent
Some sentences show **variety**, and **most** are **complete** and **generally correct**.
Surface errors are present, but they **do not interfere** with the reader's understanding.

3 = Nearly Competent
Sentences show a **little variety**, but the structure may be **dull**. Sentences are **generally complete** and grammatically correct, but **some errors** distract the reader.
Surface errors are **apparent** and **begin to interfere** with the reader's understanding of the work.

2 = Marginally Incompetent
Sentence Structure is usually simple. Problems in sentence structure and grammar distract the reader and provide little or no variety.
Surface errors are **frequent and severe enough** to **interfere** with the reader's understanding of the work.

1 = Incompetent
Sentence structure is **simple, generally erroneous** and **lacks variety**.
Surface errors are **frequent** and **extreme**, and **severely interfere** with the reader's understanding of the work.

Scoring Guide for the ACT Writing Test

WORD CHOICE

6 = Clearly Competent
The essay shows a **good command** of language. Word choice is **specific, clear**, and **vivid**, favoring **powerful nouns** and **verbs** to weaker adjective and adverb phrases. **Clear, specific words** are used, instead of vague, general terms.
The work is **free of surface errors** (grammar, spelling, punctuation, etc.).

5 = Reasonably Competent
Language is **competent**. Word choice is **clear** and **accurate**. Words and phrases are **mostly** vivid, specific, and powerful.
Minor surface errors are present, but they **do not interfere** with the reader's understanding of the work.

4 = Adequately Competent
Language is **adequate**, with **appropriate** word choice. **Most** words and phrases are vivid, specific, and powerful.
Serious surface errors are present, but they **do not interfere** with the reader's understanding.

3 = Nearly Competent
Language shows a **basic control** and word choice is **usually appropriate** but **inconsistent**.
Surface errors are **apparent** and **begin to interfere** with the reader's understanding of the work.

2 = Marginally Incompetent
Word choice is usually **vague**.
Surface errors are **frequent** and **severe enough** to **interfere** with the reader's understanding of the work.

1 = Incompetent
Word choice is **simple, vague**, and **inexact**. The writer makes **no attempt** to choose the best words for the topic, audience, and purpose.
Surface errors are **frequent** and **extreme**, and **severely interfere** with the reader's understanding of the work.

Scoring Guide for the ACT Writing Test

HOLISTIC

6 = Clearly Competent

The paper is **clearly organized** around the central idea. Ideas follow a **logical order**.

The paper **takes a position** on the issue and **offers sufficient material** (details, examples, anecdotes, supporting facts, etc.) to create a complete discussion. There is a **clear, purposed, well developed** introduction and conclusion.

The paper visits **different perspectives** of the argument or addresses **counterarguments** to the writer's position.

Sentences are **varied, complete**, and **assist the reader** in the flow of the discussion.

The paper shows a **good command** of language. Word choice is **specific, clear**, and **vivid**, favoring **powerful nouns** and **verbs** to weaker adjective and adverb phrases.

The work is **free of surface errors** (grammar, spelling, punctuation, etc.).

5 = Reasonably Competent

The organization of the paper is **clear**, but **not fully implemented**. Ideas follow a **logical order**, but transitions **might be simple** or obvious. The structure **might be predictable**.

The paper **takes a position** on the issue and **offers sufficient material** for a complete discussion, but the reader is left with **a few unanswered questions**. There is a clear **introduction** and **conclusion**.

The paper visits **some different perspectives** of the argument or addresses **counterarguments**.

Sentences are **somewhat varied, generally correct**, and **do not distract** the reader from the flow of the discussion.

Language is **competent**. Words and phrases are **mostly vivid, specific**, and **powerful**.

Minor surface errors are present, but they **do not interfere** with the reader's understanding of the work.

4 = Adequately Competent

The organization of the paper is **apparent**, but **not consistently** implemented. The structure is **predictable**. **Some** ideas follow a **logical order**, but transitions are **simple** and **obvious**. **Most** of the paper **focuses** on the topic and the specific argument.

The paper **takes a position** on the issue, but **does not provide** the details, examples, or supporting facts for a complete discussion, leaving **a few unanswered questions**.

The paper includes **little attention** to counterarguments and differing perspectives.

Irrelevant material is present.

Language is **adequate**, with appropriate word choice. **Most** words and phrases are vivid, specific, and powerful.

Some sentences show **variety**, and **most** are **complete** and **generally correct**.

Surface errors are present, but they **do not interfere** with the reader's understanding.

3 = Nearly Competent

There is **evidence of a simple organizational plan**. The essay **takes a position** on the issue but **does not include** sufficient details, examples, or supporting facts for a discussion. Ideas are **grouped logically** in parts of the paper, **but do not flow** logically throughout. The paper **focuses** on the topic, but **does not maintain** the specific argument.

The paper **may include incomplete** or **unclear** counterarguments.

Language shows a **basic control**, and word choice is **usually appropriate** but **inconsistent**. Sentences show a **little variety**, but the structure may be **dull**.

Sentences are **generally complete** and **grammatically correct**, but some errors **distract** the reader.

The paper might **repeat** details or rhetoric.

Surface errors are **apparent** and **begin to interfere** with the reader's understanding of the work.

2 = Marginally Incompetent

The organizational plan of the paper is **obscured by too few details** and/or **irrelevant details**. The paper **may not take a position** on the issue, or the paper may take a position but **fail to support** it with sufficient details. **Some** of the ideas are **grouped logically** in parts of the paper. The paper **generally maintains focus** on the general topic.

Examples and ideas are **vague** and **irrelevant**.

Sentence structure is **usually simple**. **Problems** in sentence structure and grammar **distract** the reader and provide **little** or **no variety**. **Word choice** is usually **vague**.

The paper might **repeat** ideas **extensively**.

Surface errors are **frequent and severe enough** to **interfere** with the reader's understanding of the work.

1 = Incompetent

There is **no clear organizational plan** and/or **insufficient material**. The paper **might attempt** to **take a position**, but it **fails** to provide examples, fact, or rhetoric to support the position. Ideas are **not grouped logically**.

The paper may be **repetitious** with little or **no focus** on the general topic.

Sentence structure is **simple** and **generally erroneous** and **lacking variety**. Word choice is **simple**, **vague**, and **inexact**. The writer makes **no attempt** to choose the best words for the topic, audience, and purpose.

Surface errors are **frequent** and **extreme**, and **severely interfere** with the reader's understanding of the work.

Relevant State Standards

Vocabulary Power Plus for the ACT: Book Two

High School - Grade 10

These are only the minimum standards that the product line meets; if these standards seem out of order, they typically go in "keyword" order; from the Language Usage category of standards, to Comprehension, Analysis, Writing, Research/Applied, and Technology/Media categories. Therefore these standards may be in a different order than the order given by your local Department of Education. Also if one state standard meets multiple categories, that particular standard is listed the first time it appears, to reduce redundancy. Again, please refer to your local Department of Education for details on the particular standards.

Bias/Validity standards are included, as is Voice/Style standards, as both categories include use of words for different effects on the audience (connotation, denotation, distortion, formality, etc.) and thus are logical inclusions.

Depending on state, standards pertaining to use of dialect and idiomatic expressions might be met by this product. Please refer to your local Department of Education for details.

Notation is as close as possible to the notation given by the Department of Education of the respective state.

States:

Alabama:
Std. 34; Std. 1; Std. 5; Stds. 24-28; Std. 29; Std. 9; Stds. 20-22; Std. 13; Std. 14; Std. 8; Std. 1; Std. 3; Std 4; Std. 6; Std. 23; Std. 9; Stds. 20-22

Alaska:
R4.1.1-4; R4.4.1-2; R4.5.1; R4.5.2-3; W4 (all); R4.1.5; R4.2.1-2; R4.3.1-4; R4.3.5-6; R4.7.1; R4.9.2; R4.9.1; R4.6.1-4; R4.9.1; W4.2.2; W4.4.5

Arizona:
R1.4PO1; R1.4PO2-5; R1.6PO1-5; R3.2PO1-3; R3.1PO6; R2.1PO2, 4; W1 (all); W2.4-6 (all); W2.3.1-5; R3.3PO1-3; R1.6PO1-5; R3.1PO6; R2.2PO1; R2.1PO3; W1.4PO4; W2.3.1-5

Arkansas:
R.11.10.1-4; R.10.10.1-2; R.10.10.19; R.9.10.13; W.4.10 (all); W.6.10 (all); W.5.10 (all); W.7.10.8; R.9.10.3; R.9.10.6; R.9.10.8; R9.10.4; R.10.10.24; W.4.10.13

California:
R1.1-2; R1.3; R2 (all); R3.7; R3.11; WOC1.1-5; W1.2; W2 (all); R3.12; R3.6-10; R3 (entire)

Colorado (broad standards):
S1; S6; S2; S3; S4

Connecticut:
1.3 (all); 1.1 (all); 2.1 (all); 1.2g; 3.2 (all); 4.2 (all); 4.3 (all); 3.1 (all); 1.4 (all); 2.3 (entire); 2.1D

Delaware:
2.2a; 1.5; 2.4k; 2.4bL; 4.2b; 2.4bI/T; 4.2c; 1.1; 1.3; 1.2; 1.1, 1.5; 2.4j; 2.5f; 4.3A; 2.4G; 2.3A,C; 1.3; 1.2

District of Columbia:
10.LD-V.8-10; 10.LT-G.2; 10.LT-S.10; 10.LD-Q.4; 10.W-R.6; 10.EL.1-5; 10.LT-C.1; 10.LT-F.4-5; 10.LT.TN.12-13; 10.W-E.3-5

Florida (broad standards):
R.1 (all); R.2 (all); Li.1 (all); W.1 (all); W.2.3; La.1.2; LVS.1.4; Li.1.1; Li.1 and 2

Georgia:
ELA10RC3; ELA10RL5; ELA10RL1; ELA10W1; ELA10RL4; ELA10W2;
ELA10RL3

Hawaii (broad standards):
S2; S1; S4; S5,6; S7; S3

Idaho:
10.LA.1.8.1-2; 10.LA.2.1 (all); 10.LA.4.2.3; 10.LA.2.2.2; 10.LA.1.2.2;
10.LA.2.3.5; 10.LA.3 (all); 10.LA.5.3, 4; 10.LA.4 (all); 10.LA.2.3.6;
10.LA.2.3.3; 9-12.Spch.6.3; 10.LA.2.3.4

Illinois:
1.A.4a; 1.A.4b; 1.B.4b; 1.C (all); 2.A.4d; 3.B.4b; 3.A.4; 3.B.4a; 1.B.4a; 1.B.4C;
2.B.4B; 2.A.4C; 3.B.4C

Indiana:
10.1.1-4; 10.2.3; 10.3.1; 10.2.1; 10.3.7-8; 10.4 (all); 10.6 (all); 10.5 (all);
10.3.11; 10.7.12; 10.3.12; 10.3.6; 10.3.2; 10.4.10-12

Iowa (Model Core Curriculum):
R6; R1; R3; W1; W7; W2, W3; R4; V3; R5; S7

Kansas:
RB3:1-3, 5; RB4:13; RB4:1; RB3:4; RB4:2-6, 9-10; RB4:14-15; LB1:2; RB4:11;
LB2 (entire)

Kentucky (Academic Expectations):
AE1.2; AE2.30, 33; AE2.38; AE1.11; AE6.1, 2.25

Louisiana:
RR1.1; RR1.5; RR7.12; RR6.9; W2.19; WP3.25-29; W2.20-21; W2.18; W2.24;
RR7.15; RR6.7; RR1.3; RR7.11

Maine:
A1; B7; B8, D4; A6; E1-3; F1-3; G4-5; G8; C7-8; H10-11; B5-6; B10-11; E1,4

Maryland (HAS documents used):
G3.2.2; G1.1.1-4; G1.1.5; G2.1 (all); G1.2.2-3; G3.1 (all); G3.3 (all); G2.1
(all); G1.3.3; G4.3.1; G2.3.3; G1.2.5; G1.2.4

Massachusetts:
4.23; 4.24; 4.25; 13.25; 15.7; 21.8; 5.23-28; 22.9; 25.5; 19.25; 20.5; 6.8-9;

24.5; 9.6; 8.29; 10.5; 3.16

Michigan (Michigan Merit Curriculum used):
3.3; 3.2; 1.1; 4.1; 1.3, 1.5; 2.1, 2.2; 2.3

Minnesota:
IB4-5; IB1-5; ID14; IC3; ID9; IC4; ID4-5; IIB1-8; IIC2-3; IIA1; IIC1; IIIB5-7, 9-10; IC8; ID15; ID1-3; ID12; IIIA7

Mississippi:
1a; 2a-d; 2e; 1b-d; 3a; 4a-c; 3b-d; 1B; 1C

Missouri:
I5c; II2b; III1; I6a-d; II3c; IV2d; I1c; III1a; I1a; II1b; II4a, c-h; II6a-b; III1a; II3a-b; I5B; I4A,C; II1D; II3A; II3A-B

Montana:
RCS2; RCS1; LCS1; RCS5; WCS2; WCS1; WCS4; RCS4; RCS3; LCS2; LCS5

Nebraska (standards set at grade 12):
12.1.1; 12.1.5; 12.1.6

Nevada (standards set at grade 12):
1.12.3; 1.12.4-5; 2.12.1-3; 4.12.6; 5.12.2; 3.12.7; 3.12.5-6; 6.12.1-5, 7; 7.12.1-5; 5.12.2-6; 3.12.3; 3.12.1; 8.12.2

New Hampshire:
R-10-1, 2, 3; R-10-13; R-10-7.1-3; R-10-4.4; R-10-7.5; R-10-4.5; R-10-6.1; W-10-10; W-10-1, 9; W-10-11.4; R-10-15.2; R-10-11.1-3

New Jersey:
3.1.F.1-3; 3.1.G.12-13; 3.2.D.6; 3.1.D.3; 3.2.B.1; 3.1.G.11; 3.1.G.6; 3.1.G.8; 3.2.A (all); 3.2.C (all); 3.2.B.5; 3.2.B.1; 3.2.D.2; 3.2.D.8; 3.1.E.1-3; 3.1.G.9; 3.1.H.6; 3.4.B.2-3; 3.5.B.1; 3.1.G.3; 3.1.G.5; 3.1.G.7; 3.2.A.6-7

New Mexico:
1C10-3; 3B10-3; 2A10 (all); 1C10-2; 3B10-1,2; 1A10-4; 2A10 (entire)

New York (broad standards):
ELA-S1, ELA-S2; ELA-S3

North Carolina:
6.01; 1.03; 2.01; 4.05; 6.01-02; 4.04

North Dakota:
10.2.1; 10.2.4; 10.6.2-3; 10.3.3-14; 10.6.1; 10.2.2; 10.6.5; 10.3.8

Ohio:
10-WC; 10-RP; 10-RA-IT; 10-RA-L; 10-WP; 10-WC; 10-WA

Oklahoma:
10-RL1 (all); 10-RL2-4c; 10-RL3-1a-b; 10-RL3-3a-c; 10-WM1 (all); 10-WM3 (all); 10-WM2 (all); 10-RL2-1c; 10-VL1-1; 10-RL2-1b, 4b; 10-RL3-4A; 10-RL3-2D-E; 10-RL3-4C; 10-WM1-6; 10-WM2-7C,8

Oregon:
EL.CM.RE.08-14; EL.CM.RE.15-18; EL.CM.RE.02; EL.CM.LI.13; EL.CM. WR.01-09; EL.CM.WR.10-20; EL.CM.WR.21-26; EL.CM.SL.01-09; EL.CM. RE.06; EL.CM.RE.27, 28, 31; EL.CM.LI.01; EL.CM.LI.11-14; EL.CM.LI.17-18; EL.CM.WR.07

Pennsylvania (standards set at grade 11):
1.1.11C; 1.1.11E-F; 1.1.11G; 1.1.11H; 1.1.11B; 1.3.11C; 1.5.11 (all); 1.4.11 (all); 1.1.11D; 1.3.11B; 1.4.11D-E

Rhode Island:
R-10-1, 2, 3; R-10-13; R-10-7.1-3; R-10-4.4; R-10-7.5; R-10-4.5; R-10-6.1; W-10-10; W-10-1, 9; W-10-11.4; R-10-15.2; R-10-11.1-3

South Carolina:
E2-R3.1-4; E2-R2.2; E2-R1.3; E2-W1.6.2-5; E2-R1.5; E2-R2.2, 4; E2-W1 (all); E2-W1.6.1; E2-W2 (all); E2-R1.7-9; E2-C3.7; E2-R1.4; E2-R2.1; E2-R5-6; E2-R2.3,6; E2-C1.13

South Dakota:
10.W.1.2; 10.R.2.2; 10.W.1.1; 10.W.3.1; 10.R.4.1-2; 10.R.3.1; 10.R.2.1

Tennessee (Learning Expectations):
2LE-3; 2LE-1; 4LE-10; 1LE-1; 2LE-4, 5, 8; 2LE-13; 2LE-14; 1LE- 5-10; 1LE-11; 1LE-2, 3, 4; 2LE-10; 2.2.E

Texas (TEKS section 110.43):
b6 (all); b7 (all); b8B; b11D; b12A; b2 (all); b3 (all); b12B-C; B8D; B9A; B11A,F; B5 (entire)

Utah:
1-O1 (all); 1-O2 (all); 1-O3e; 2-O3 (all); 3-O1c; 1-03a,e; 1-03 (entire)

Vermont:
R-10-1, 2, 3; R-10-13; R-10-7.1-3; R-10-4.4; R-10-7.5; R-10-4.5; R-10-6.1;
W-10-10; W-10-1, 9; W-10-11.4; R-10-15.2; R-10-11.1-3

Virginia:
10.4; 10.3; 10.7; 10.8; 10.3D; 10.9

Washington (EALRs used here):
R1.2; R2 (all); R3 (all); W2.4; W1 (all); W3.3; W2 (all); W3.2; W4.1

West Virginia (prefix for these citations: RLA):
O.10.1.10; O.10.1.04-06, 09; O.10.1.02; O.10.1.07; O.10.2.01-10; O.10.1.11;
O.10.1.01; O.10.1.08

Wisconsin (standards set at grade 12):
D.12.1; A.12.1; A.12.4; A.12.2; B.12.2; B.12.3; B.12.1; A.12.2-3

Wyoming:
R-IB; R-IA; R-IIIB2; R-IIA; R-IIIA; R-IIC; W-IB; W-IE, F, G; W-IA; W-IIA;
W-IIB; W-IIC; W-IID; W-ID; SL-1b; R-IIB2,5; SL-9